CW01429085

THE
LITTLE
HISTORY
OF
GALWAY

THE
LITTLE
HISTORY
OF
GALWAY

COLM WALLACE

First published 2024

The History Press
97 St George's Place, Cheltenham,
Gloucestershire, GL50 3QB
www.thehistorypress.co.uk

British Library Cataloguing in Publication Data.
A catalogue record for this book is available from the British Library.

ISBN 978 1 80399 707 0

Typesetting and origination by The History Press
Printed and bound in Great Britain by TJ Books Limited, Padstow, Cornwall.

CONTENTS

ABOUT THE AUTHOR

Colm Wallace is a native of Renvyle, Co. Galway. Married with four children, he works as a school teacher and has completed a Masters in History at the University of Galway. This is his third book.

INTRODUCTION

County Galway lies on the west coast of the island of Ireland and stretches from the Atlantic Ocean in the west to Lough Derg and the River Suck in the east, comprising a total area of approximately 6,100 sq km, the second largest county in Ireland by size. As of 2024, it was home to a population of more than 276,000 people, making it the fifth largest of Ireland's thirty-two counties by population. The origin of Galway's name is uncertain, although it may come from the Irish words *gall* and *amh* meaning 'stony river'. The area we now call Galway was shired by the English in 1569, becoming an official county. Along with counties Mayo, Roscommon, Sligo and Leitrim, Galway is situated in the western province of Connacht, the region that features most of the territory of Ireland west of the River Shannon. Galway's coat of arms comprises a hooker, a fishing boat synonymous with the county, with five stars in the sky around it. Its motto is the Irish language phrase *Ceart agus Cóir*, which means 'right and just'.

The county is divided into three distinct areas in terms of culture and topography. The rugged western end of County Galway is the region known as Connemara, a largely Irish-speaking area famed for its uplands, both the Twelve Bens and Maamturk Mountains looming large. The larger of the two ranges is the Twelve Bens (*Na Beanna Beola*), named after a mythological giant, Beola, and rising to 729m at

A Currach to the Aran Islands (from *On an Irish Jaunting Car* by Samuel Bayne).

Benbaun, Galway's highest point. Connemara is also home to hundreds of lakes, including most of the second largest freshwater lake on the island of Ireland, Lough Corrib. Lough Corrib is 68 sq miles and runs north-west from Galway City, through Connemara and into Co. Mayo. It is home to hundreds of islands, several of which have ecclesiastical and historical ruins, most notably Inchagoill. Lough Mask is also one of the largest lakes in Ireland, although only about half the size of Lough Corrib, and it too is partially situated in Connemara. Several islands have the ruins of ancient buildings, most notably the Church of St Cormac on Inishmaan. The largest lake entirely situated in Co. Galway, Lough Inagh, is also in Connemara. The largest Gaeltacht (Irish-speaking area) in Ireland also lies in Connemara and features such villages as Leitir Mór, Cheathrú Rua, Carna, Ros Muc, An Spidéal, Indreabhán as well as na hOileáin Árainn (the Aran Islands).

Connemara retains a distinct identity within the county, and although its boundaries are loosely defined, it is generally considered to be all the land in Co. Galway west of the villages of Moycullen and Barna. The main town is Clifden, known widely as the capital of Connemara, and the region borders only Co. Mayo to the north, being surrounded by the ocean on all other sides. Most of Galway's 700km coastline is in Connemara and it is peppered with dozens of offshore islands, including four that remain permanently inhabited: Inishbofin and the three Aran Islands, Inishmore, Inishmaan and Inisheer. Several other formerly offshore islands have been bridged in the last century and a half, and now have a connection with the mainland, including Lettermore, Inishnee and Gorumna. In consequence of this unique geography, Connemara is sparsely populated, with nearly all of its 32,000 inhabitants living in scattered villages along the coast. The interior is boggy, mountainous and largely devoid of roads. The area is famed for its beauty, however, and it is much visited by tourists.

The second distinct region of County Galway is Galway City, which lies in the centre of the county, just to the east of Connemara, where Lough Corrib becomes the 6km River Corrib. The River Corrib acted as a handy crossing point in medieval times and a settlement grew around it for this reason. Originally called *Baile an Srutháin* (the town of the streams), it would in later times come to be known as Galway City. Today, the city has a population of more than 80,000 people and is comfortably the largest urban centre in the western province of Connacht. There is also a large population in the suburbs and just outside the city limits, particularly in the rapidly growing towns such as Claregalway, Craughwell and Oranmore on its eastern edge. Consequently, the city is a centre for employment and is home to many industries, most notably those involved in the manufacture of medical devices. It is known as a hub for arts and culture, and tourists also flock to Galway City, which has a scenic seaside location and a bustling nightlife. It has nevertheless maintained much of its medieval charm and is a popular destination for people interested in history.

The third region of the county is centred around east and south Galway, a largely flat limestone region that is characterised by fertile lands, pleasant villages and rich, low-lying pastures. Along with large stretches of prime agricultural land, this region's topography also comprises thousands of acres of raised bogs that were traditionally used for turf cutting. Several rivers of note, including the Clare, the Clarin and the Suck, flow through east Galway, the latter draining much of the land in the region. Lough Derg, the third biggest lake in Ireland, is to the south-east. The south of the county shares a long border with Clare, while the east has shorter borders with both Co. Offaly and Co. Tipperary. There is a far longer border with Co. Roscommon to the east and north of the county. Although the region is flat, it does have the low-lying Slieve Aughty Mountains, which stretch from Loughrea to Gort in the west and Mountshannon in Co. Clare in the south-east. Their highest point is Cashlaundrumlahan, at 400m.

There is also the Esker Riada, a line of gravel hills that extend from Clarinbridge all the way through the middle of the county and onwards through Leinster. In ancient times, this ridge formally marked the border between the south and the north of Ireland. Farming is an important facet of life here and tourists are less likely to happen upon the pleasant market towns and villages that dot the landscape. South and east Galway are known for being suited to the planting of most crops, although the low-lying land is regularly flooded in the winter months. Athenry, Portumna, Loughrea, Tuam and Ballinasloe are among the largest urban centres in the east Galway region, and while traditionally they were market towns catering for the farming community in their hinterland, today they are thriving and growing centres, many acting as commuter towns for Galway.

All three regions have had storied human histories going back thousands of years. Together, these form the history of the county of Galway.

1

GALWAY: EARLY HISTORY, CHRISTIANITY AND MYTHOLOGY

THE STONE AGE

The mountains of Galway formed more than 500 million years ago and, as the last Ice Age retreated, the melting glaciers deposited soil and sand and the varied topography of the area began to take shape. The warming climate that followed allowed plants, flowers and trees to bloom. By 8000 BC, we know that there were communities of people on the island of Ireland. Little is known of these pre-Celtic people and how they lived, although they seem to have arrived on the isolated island long after the rest of southern Europe was populated. Ireland's wet climate may have been somewhat uninviting, but the tree-covered island with abundant water and devoid of people must have seemed like fertile hunting and fishing territory all the same. The first people probably arrived to the north of the country from Scotland, spreading southwards and westwards over time. They were able to get food by hunting animals and birds, catching fish and eating the nuts and berries that they could pick off the trees and bushes. They were called hunter-gatherers.

They generally travelled around rather than living in permanent settlements, spending time along the coasts and near rivers and lakes, where they erected temporary wooden huts with roofs made from rushes or animal skins.

The first known habitation of the area now known as Co. Galway was in around 6000 BC, with artefacts found in the rivers around Galway City seeming to suggest human activity at this time. Galway had many water sources and these early people chose to settle along the coasts, rivers and lakes of the county. Examples of shell middens dating back to around 5000 BC can be found in western coastal regions of Connemara, notably on the Slyne Head peninsula, while the watery depths of Lough Corrib have produced many artefacts, including log boats and Stone Age tools, which can today be traced to prehistoric times.

In around 4000 BC, new ideas arrived from Europe that were to revolutionise life in Galway and its surrounds. This is now known as the Neolithic Age or New Stone Age. Agricultural practices that we now recognise as farming

Lough Corrib (from *Sunny Side of Ireland* by John O'Mahony).

had been practised in Europe for generations and these settlers in the New Stone Age were able to cultivate crops and cereals and raise domesticated animals such as cattle and sheep. This prompted people to give up their nomadic lifestyle and set down roots, giving Galway its first taste of settled communities. At this time, Galway was covered in forestry but large-scale tree felling using primitive stone tools began. These first farmers, despite their lack of technology, built walls, cleared fields and used local materials to build more permanent houses.

Many Neolithic sites can be found in Galway, particularly in west Connemara and on the shores of Lough Corrib. There are also several Neolithic tombs on the sacred hill of Knockma near Tuam. Burial customs were obviously important to the people of the New Stone Age and there are many megalithic tombs in Co. Galway. The area around Lough Sheeauns near Cleggan, in north-west Connemara, shows much evidence of these, while a collapsed megalithic tomb near Menlo, just east of Galway City, is also a prime example. Portal tombs can also be found in Renvyle and Clifden. Fragments from the time, including handmade pottery, have also been discovered and examined by archaeologists. Axe heads, including a well-preserved specimen from Monivea, have been recovered, as have other cutting tools made from porcellanite. Some of these are on display in the National Museum of Ireland, others in Galway City Museum.

THE BRONZE AGE

The Bronze Age, which began in around 2500 BC, was a truly revolutionary period. Irish people had been using copper for generations, and although it was mainly associated with the south of the country, it could also be found underground in Co. Galway. Copper itself was useful but the discovery in south-east Europe that mixing it with tin at high heat made a durable metal called bronze changed the world, this new metal allowing the manufacture of stronger tools and weapons that made farming and the clearing of land far easier. It would take several hundred years before such a practice became commonplace in Ireland, however. This was because there was no tin to speak of on the island and it needed to be imported from countries such as England. The precious metal was used for more than tools, however – the Bronze Age eventually became synonymous with ornamental items and jewellery, and gold lunulas are among the decorative items that have been found in the area around Galway.

During the Bronze Age, houses were made of wattle and daub or wood, and cooking was often done in an open-air pit known as a *fulacht fiadh*, examples of which can be found in Galway, including at Eyrecourt. Burial practices also changed in the Bronze Age and single burials in pit graves became common, the bodies of wealthier individuals often accompanied by impressive items such as crockery or jewellery. The grave was usually marked by a mound. There are several examples of this type of burial in Co. Galway, particularly around the Cleggan area to the west. Cist graves – small, stone-built, coffin-like boxes used to hold the bodies of the dead – were common too and can be found in several locations between Athenry to Headford. Stone circles and standing stones were also prevalent, the modern belief being that these were settings for important pagan ceremonies and rituals. A well-preserved example of a standing stone can be found at Roscam on Galway Bay and there are several others present throughout Connemara and near Lough Corrib. There are also examples of stone circles, including in the townland of Moanmore West, near Loughrea, and at Commons East near Woodford, the latter of which consists of seven free-standing stones.

THE COMING OF THE CELTS

The Bronze Age in Ireland came to an end in around 500 BC, having lasted about 1,500 years. At this stage, a group of people known as the Celts arrived in Ireland from mainland Europe. They brought with them new skills and talents to further improve the island. The well-preserved body of an adult male from Celtic times was found in 1821 near Castleblakeney in Co. Galway. The boots he was wearing were a good example of the ingenuity of the Celtic race. Portions of the seams remained and indicated an impressive understanding of stitchwork. The Celts' arrival also coincided with the discovery of a new metal – iron. Iron did not need to be mixed like bronze and was thus easier to obtain. Iron tools were also very strong and durable and before long had replaced bronze tools, marking the beginning of the Iron Age. The Celts were not an entirely peaceful race and iron weapons were also a feature. It is difficult to ascertain how much violence heralded their arrival, but swords and spearheads dating from Celtic times have been discovered in Co. Galway, particularly on the shores of the River Suck, indicating that they did not always come in peace.

By the time of the Celts' arrival, the people of Galway were living in small communities, often built strategically on hilltops to provide protection. Cows were the main symbol of wealth and land was prized above anything else. Feuding was a reality of life and *crannógs*, artificial defensive islands in the centre of lakes, were built widely, including at Lough Caimin near Roundstone, Lough Skannive near Carna and

Lough Acalla near Kilconnell in east Galway. There were also several in the lake at Loughrea. Other types of forts were built in Ireland for protection and shelter in and before Celtic times. Promontory forts were built on cliffs and jutted out into the sea. Dún Aonghasa on the Aran Islands is one of the finest examples of these in the world. Hillforts were made of stone and built on high land overlooking the surrounding countryside, and there is an excellent example of one of these near Lough na Fooey in Joyce Country, Co. Galway. Ringforts, too, were commonly built and often comprised several houses together in small communities, surrounded by circular stone walls for protection. These are particularly common in the rich farmland landscape in the east of the county and examples can be seen at Woodlawn and New Inn.

Proximity to water sources remained important and the area now home to Galway City, which was an ideal crossing point of the River Corrib, may have had its first major settlement at this time. The Celts were capable fishermen too, and in 1820, James Hardiman stated that:

> The town of Gallway was formerly inhabited by colonies, who got their livelyhood by cods & other sea fishes, drying them by the sun. No part of the Irish coast abounds with a greater variety of fish.[1]

Celts were skilled ironmongers and were able to clear land of trees, build small settlements and grow crops, which they used to make bread and porridge. Some of the techniques in farming introduced at this time were so advanced that they are still used today. The Celts also domesticated many animals, including cows and pigs, and consumed

---

1   Hardiman, J. (1820), *The History of the Town and County of the Town of Galway*, p.5.

dairy products such as milk, butter and cheese. Their strong iron tools allowed them to experiment with new methods of building houses as well. They brought more advanced methods of thatching their roofs, tying rushes and straw together skilfully to make a roof in such a way that would keep a house warm and dry. The houses were usually made of wood or stone. They also sometimes had a souterrain, an underground passage for storing food or occasionally hiding from enemies. A great example of this can be seen at Ballynastaig stone fort, near Gort, while another has been discovered at Carnmore. They were also skilled craftsmen, as the Turoe Stone, found at Bullaun near Loughrea, attests. It is a granite carved stone with beautiful artwork, the meaning of which has been lost to time but is nevertheless a reminder of Galway's rich Celtic past.

CHRISTIAN GALWAY

Over the following centuries, the Celts and the original Irish settlers intermarried and became indistinguishable. By the fourth century, however, a new force was on its way to Ireland. Christianity had its origins in the Middle East, slowly spreading to Europe. In AD 381, it became the official religion of the Roman Empire and it spread rapidly throughout the continent thereafter. The Celts had been pagans and had worshipped many gods and goddesses that they believed were in natural objects such as the sea, the sky and the sun. Some of the most revered goddesses, for example, included Morrigan, the Goddess of War; Danu, the Goddess of Power; and Brigit, the Goddess of Fire. The Irish would have been largely unfamiliar with Christianity until several decades into the fifth century. Many people believe that the first missionary to attempt to spread Christianity in

Ireland was a bishop named Palladias, but our patron saint, St Patrick, is widely considered to have converted much of the country, even if hard evidence about his life in Ireland is hard to come by.

Kidnapped from his home, possibly in Wales, Patrick worked as a slave minding sheep for several years, possibly in Co. Antrim. After escaping from his captors and training as a bishop, Patrick returned to Ireland in AD 432 to spread Christianity. It is said he used the three leaves of the Shamrock, which grows widely in Ireland, to teach the pagan Irish about the Father, the Son and the Holy Spirit, and succeeded in converting many important chiefs, who in turn urged their people to embrace the new religion. The influence of Christianity would be felt strongly within years of his arrival. Patrick visited Galway on numerous occasions. He is said to have travelled around north Galway speaking to local chieftains and attempting to convert them, and St Patrick's Bed, an altar where the saint was said to have prayed, is located near Tuam.

S. PATRICIVS HIBERNIÆ APOSTOLVS
Claruit Anno Domini CCCCLVIII.

The Saint Patrick of Mediæval Times.

Another important destination for St Patrick was *Mám Éan* (Maumeen), a hill in the Inagh Valley overlooking Connemara. He is said to have stood atop the mountain and blessed the region. A pattern day on one Sunday each summer to celebrate

St Patrick (from *The Most Ancient Lives of Saint Patrick* by James O'Leary).

this event was popular for centuries, but by the twenti-eth century had dwindled in significance compared to its more famous rival of Croagh Patrick in Co. Mayo. In more recent years, thanks largely to the work of Fr Micheál Mac Gréil and the local community, the pilgrimage is once again thriving and a small chapel and statue dedicated to the saint have been built on the hill. The oldest still extant Christian church in Ireland is reputedly situated at Kiltiernan, Co. Galway. The building survives from the eighth century, but there is evidence of worship even earlier, possibly from the fifth century when Patrick himself walked among us. St Patrick died in AD 461 and was said to have been buried at Downpatrick, Co. Down.

THE LAND OF SAINTS AND SCHOLARS

This coming of Christianity in the fifth century ushered in a golden age for Irish education and the island eventu-ally became known as the Land of Saints and Scholars. Monasteries were constructed all over the country, usually in isolated areas where the monks could live and pray in peace. The monasteries were skilfully built using stone and usually had a round tower, a guest house, a scriptorium, and many other impressive buildings. They were often led by a revered saint and many young monks were schooled in the arts of reading and writing, usually by using the Bible. Beautiful manuscripts were printed on vellum by the young monks, the most famous of which is the Book of Kells. Numerous intact examples of such monasteries can still be seen in Co. Galway, including at Kilmacduagh and Clonfert.

The Aran Islands were also home to one such monastery. *Na Oileáin Árainn*, as they are called in Irish, are situ-ated off the coast of Galway at the mouth of Galway Bay.

They comprise 47 sq km in total and are made up of three islands: Inishmore, Inishmaan and Inisheer. Enda, who had been a soldier and the son of a prince from Ulster, repented from his life of violence and after ordination in Rome chose to go to the windswept western outpost of Inishmore, the largest of the three islands, where he founded what may have been Ireland's first monastery. The monks in this monastery lived a hard life of work, prayer, fasting and studying scriptures, and several went on to found their own monasteries. It is said that when Enda died, he was buried at the church at *Cill Éinne* (the Church of Enda) on the island, and there are reputed to be dozens of other saints in the same graveyard, which can be visited to this day.

Another famous saint who made Galway his home was St Brendan, who founded a monastery at Clonfert in the extreme east of the county in the middle of the sixth century. Born in Co. Kerry in the year AD 484, Brendan is most famed as 'Brendan the Navigator', many believing he discovered America centuries before Christopher Columbus. Clonfert was renowned for the learning that occurred there and it

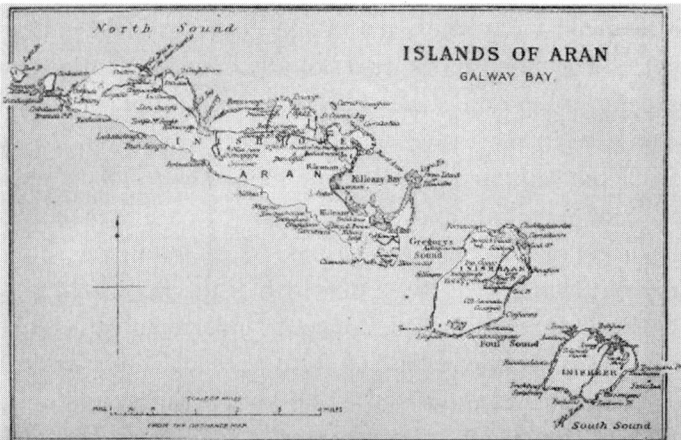

The Aran Islands (from *Ireland's Ancient Schools and Scholars* by John Healy).

thrived for centuries. Like many monasteries, however, a Viking raid would eventually bring it to its knees and it was burned down on at least three occasions. St Brendan is said to be buried in the churchyard adjoining the cathedral.

Kilmacduagh is another famous monastery in Galway. Its name comes from the Irish *Cill Mhic Dhuach*, meaning 'Church of Colman mac Duagh'. It is exceptionally well preserved to this day and is situated on the outskirts of the limestone landscape of the Burren, a region synonymous with Co. Clare but which has a small section inside the Galway border. Founded in the seventh century by St Colman, Kilmacduagh was a hugely important site by 1100. Like all monasteries, it eventually declined in importance when the Irish Church came under the banner of the Church of Rome, but a pattern fair celebrating St Colman was popular at Kilmacduagh for centuries. Other saints synonymous with Galway include St MacDara of Carna, St Grellan of Ballinasloe, St Caillín of Ballyconneely and St Fursey of Inchiquin Island. St Jarlath was also an important saint, founding the town of Tuam in the sixth century after his chariot broke its wheel there and he took it as a sign from God that this was the place he should make his home. Tuam went on to become Galway's most important centre of population for centuries.

MYTHOLOGICAL GALWAY

Galway is also associated with many legends of pre-Christian origin. There is even a mythological theory as to how Galway got its name, concerning a woman, Gaillimh Iníon Breasail, daughter of a local chieftain, who was said to have drowned in the Rover Corrib but whose existence is uncertain. Hy-Brasil, a strange and mysterious land, was said to be located in the sea off the county's coast. It was believed that it appeared every seven years and it was even recorded on several maps in medieval times.

Irish heroes of mythology, including Fionn Mac Cumhaill, are also said to have spent time in Galway. One story tells of how the warrior was hunting in the Twelve Bens mountains when he spotted a deer. Not knowing it was his mortal enemy who had turned himself into an animal, Fionn and his hound chased the deer to a dark valley near Duchrú Mountain, where the deer jumped over a precipice into the middle of a lake. The hound, believing his prey to be escaping, also took a desperate jump but was dashed on the rocks below. Meanwhile, the deer reached the other bank and made his escape up the mountainside. The foul deed did not benefit this evil-minded man, however, as shortly afterwards he was killed in a battle against Fionn and his men. There remains a townland in the Kylemore area named Lemnaheltia to this day. It comes from the Irish *Léim na hÉilte*, translating as 'the leap of the doe'.

Fionn Mac Cumhaill (from *The High Deeds of Finn* by T.W. Rolleston).

Many other stories of folklore are concerned with Connemara. Fionn was also said to have slain a terrible beast at the mouth of Killary Harbour that had come to kill him and the rest of his band of knights. Even Connemara's name comes from an Irish legend, *Conmaicne Mara* (Conmac of the Sea). He was a mysterious figure who may have been the son of the legendary Queen Maeve of Connacht. Queen Maeve herself was said by some sources to be buried at Knockma Hill, 8km west of Tuam, although other sources believe she is buried at Knocknarea in Co. Sligo. Knockma Hill was also said to be the place where Finvarra, the King of the Fairies of Connacht, regularly held his court. The *Tuath Dé Dannan*, a supernatural race that resided in the 'Otherworld' but that were also able to interact with those living in the 'Real World', were also said to have visited Galway on occasion, their fearsome leader Orbsen (also known as Manannán mac Lir) reputedly dying in battle in Moycullen and giving his name to nearby Lough Corrib. The Slieve Aughty Mountains are said to take their name from Echtge, a relative of Finde of the *Tuatha Dé Danann*. There are also several places in Galway named *Leaba Diarmaid agus Grainne* (Diarmaid and Gráinne's bed) for the couple from Irish mythology who ran around the country attempting to escape Gráinne's spurned lover.

2

THE VIKINGS, THE NORMANS AND THE TRIBES OF GALWAY

THE VIKINGS

By the ninth century, Galway was divided into several Gaelic *tuaths* or kingdoms. The boundaries of these were often loosely defined and ever changing, but in Galway they included Conmaince Mara to the west (later Connemara), Uí Maine to the east and Uí Fiachrach Aidnhe to the south. These kingdoms were ruled by different families and the alliances between them were regularly in flux. Battles for supremacy and for territory were waged regularly. None foresaw an even more frightening foe arriving to Irish shores: the Vikings. Also known as the Norsemen, the Vikings came from Scandinavia and were skilled farmers who desired good land. The lack of availability of such farmland in their home countries, as well as Scandinavia's harsh climate with its long, dark winters, encouraged them to travel overseas. The Vikings' first foray into Ireland was their attack on Lambay Island, Co. Dublin, in about AD 795. There was a monastery on the island and the Vikings made off with its valuables after violently raiding it and killing many monks. Galway, as a coastal region, was always

likely to be targeted and within little over a decade Viking
longships would be seen coming on the horizon to the west.

The first Viking raid on Co. Galway was probably conducted on the area around Oranmore in AD 807. Little is
known of what exactly transpired but Vikings returned
in 835, James Hardiman noting that in that year they
destroyed Galway City. They came on other occasions that
have been lost to history as well; the burial site of a ninth-
century Viking warrior, with his sword, shield and spear,
was discovered in the 1940s at Eyrephort, near Clifden.
What caused his death, and how he came to be buried there,
is impossible to tell at this juncture. Monasteries were particularly attractive to Vikings and Kilmacduagh was sacked
twice in the ninth century. It was not only the Vikings who
plundered the riches of Galway monasteries, however.
Clonfert Abbey was sacked by an army of the O'Rourke
clan in the eleventh century. It was Vikings who inspired
the most fear, however, and yet another attack from the

A Viking Expedition (from *Myths of the Norsemen* by H.A. Guerber).

'foreigners of Limerick' in AD 927 was a crippling blow to the village on the site of the present-day Galway City. On this occasion, the Norsemen ventured further inland, sacking monastic sites on several important islands on Lough Corrib. In 2014, Viking weapons, including battleaxes with intact wooden handles, an iron axe and two spearheads, were found in a well-preserved state at the bottom of Lough Corrib, alongside a longship.

The memory of Vikings and their exploits lived on in Galway for centuries. In 1796, a Frenchman named Chevalier de Lotocnaye visited the far west of Connemara, remarking:

> This country along the coast would seem to have been inhabited a long time ago. Often there are marks of furrows in places where the inhabitants have no recollection whatever of cultivation, and here, where there is no knowledge or tradition, the work is attributed to the Danes. The ancient cultivation of this country has been the work of an intelligent people; whoever they were, they have drained peat mosses of considerable size and cultivated them.[2]

Eventually, resistance to the marauding Vikings was organised and the clans of Galway, which included the O'Halloran, O'Connor and O'Flaherty families, began to defend their settlements. In AD 938, a band of Vikings was defeated in a battle near Kiltartan. The Battle of Clontarf, which took place in Co. Dublin, in 1014, was another bloody encounter with far-reaching consequences. Alliances were complicated but it was largely a fight between the Vikings, and some of their allies from Leinster, against most of the rest of the native Irish under Brian Boru, the High King of Ireland from Munster. The battle featured several Galway luminaries including Mael Ruanaidh Ua hEidhin

2   De Lotocnaye, C. (1797), *A Frenchman's Walk through Ireland*, p.171.

of Uí Fiachrach Aidhne and Tadhg Ua Ceallaigh of Uí Maine. It resulted in something of a victory for the Irish, although many of their leaders were killed, including Brian Boru himself. After this point, relations slowly began to improve between the Vikings and the native Irish and inter-marriage between the two groups gradually grew common. Eventually, the two groups became indistinguishable. The site of present-day Galway City struggled to recover from its repeated pummelling at the hands of the Vikings, however, and Hardiman stated that as late as the eleventh century the settlement 'had been reduced to the state of a miserable village, consisting of a few straggling huts inhabited by fishermen and their families'.

In the centuries after the Battle of Clontarf, Ireland's complicated system of kingdoms saw many changes, with tuaths uniting to consolidate their power. Galway was in the western kingdom of Connacht and was itself subdi-vided, the O'Flahertys further to the west rivalling the O'Connors to the east as one of the most important fami-lies. The O'Connors resided in the town of Tuam, which was far more important than Galway City at this point and was designated as the ecclesiastical headquarters of Connacht, which for a brief period was considered Ireland's foremost province. During the eleventh and twelfth centu-ries, Tuam became a thriving medieval religious town. At least two impressive High Crosses were constructed, while an ornamental gold cross was also crafted that was said to hold a relic of the true cross on which Jesus Christ was cru-cified. A stone castle was built in the town in 1161, one of the first of its kind in Ireland.

The town at the mouth of Lough Corrib remained strate-gically important as well, however, and in 1124 the Gaelic lord of Connacht, Turlough O'Connor, built a heavily forti-fied settlement at Galway. Even though the Viking threat had receded, the O'Connors had to be constantly vigilant to the threat of attack and there remained shifting alliances between the various kingdoms. Connacht was regularly at war with Leinster, Ulster or Munster. In 1133, the O'Connors' fortress at Dunmore was attacked by the Desmonds and O'Briens of Munster and Cathal O'Connor was killed. Turlough O'Brien, King of Munster, invaded Connacht yet again through south Galway in 1149 and destroyed the town and castle of Galway. These fights between the various kingdoms continued at regular intervals until late in the twelfth century, when another unexpected enemy came to the gates.

THE NORMANS

The coming of the Normans was preceded by Connacht joining forces with the kingdom of Breifne, situated in modern-day Cavan and Leitrim, in the 1160s. Their combined army took on Leinster, the eastern kingdom. Leinster was roundly defeated, forcing its king Diarmuid MacMurrough to go into exile in England. MacMurrough did not wish to lose his territory and went to the court of King Henry II, begging for his help to regain his lost lands. The king was not then prepared to be directly involved in an Irish quarrel but the subjugation of the island seemed an attractive prospect nonetheless. For this reason, MacMurrough was directed to enlist the aid of some Norman lords from south Wales. The Normans had been the inhabitants of the area around Normandy in modern-day France and were renowned as powerful soldiers. They invaded England and, in 1066, they won the Battle of Hastings against the natives. The Normans ruled England for a century and had little to do with the Irish, until Diarmuid MacMurrough's overture to King Henry II brought them into direct contact.

One of these lords, Strongbow (Richard de Clare), agreed to assist in the invasion of Ireland, if he could marry MacMurrough's daughter, Aoife, and inherit the kingdom of Leinster on Diarmuid's death. This was agreed and Strongbow led a party of Normans into Ireland after landing in Co. Wexford in 1167. The island would never be the same again. On arriving in Wexford, they quickly overran the south-east and made their way to Dublin. Many men from Galway rushed to Dublin and joined forces with other native Irish clans to try to prevent the Normans taking the capital but, led by Strongbow and possessing superior fighting tactics and powerful weapons like crossbows, the Norman soldiers proved formidable and managed to subjugate the town. They spread westwards, building huge castles for defence in their occupied territories. Some Irish towns did attempt to fight the Normans in the early stages, although it quickly became apparent that they faced overwhelming odds and many sued for peace.

Connacht managed to remain free of Normans for several decades and retain its independence. Rory O'Connor of Tuam would be the last High King of Ireland, however. He signed a treaty with the Normans in 1175 that gave him full control over the western part of the island. This made him high king in name only and the Normans were quick to break the pact, attempting invasions of Connacht in 1177 and 1188, both of which were repulsed. The death of O'Connor at Cong in 1198 marked the beginning of the end of Connacht's resistance, although his brother Cathal ascended to the throne and attempted to make terms with the Normans. The Normans, however, prized good agricultural land, defensive potential and proximity to water. Modern-day County Galway had many places with such attributes and Galway City was particularly suitable on all counts. By the beginning of the thirteenth century, Cathal

O'Connor was paying King John £200 to continue to be allowed reign over Connacht, making him a vassal king. Norman troops had already taken Athlone, just over the River Shannon from Connacht, and the possession of Galway and its environs was clearly one of their aims. In 1215, the Crown granted a Norman lord named Richard de Burgo the land of Connacht on the condition that he did not attempt to seize it until after Cathal O'Connor's death. After this came to pass in 1224, it was only a matter of time before the full force of the Norman forces was unleashed.

In 1230, under the leadership of said Richard de Burgo, Norman forces crossed the Shannon and took east Galway with relative ease. They eventually massed on the east bank of the River Corrib, where they were met by an army featuring soldiers from the O'Connor and O'Flaherty clans. The Gaelic Irish tribes fought bravely against great odds and held their own, forcing a Norman retreat. There were several more battles until 1235, when the Normans were finally able to take the strategic territory. They then built a castle on modern-day Flood Street near the banks of the River Corrib and claimed the area around Galway City as their own. They built another impressive defensive castle at Loughrea in 1236 and a third in Athenry three years later to further copper-fasten their hold on the eastern end of the county. Towns grew around both structures, although each was attacked on several occasions by the disgruntled native Irish.

The Normans ultimately went on to station garrisons in Claregalway, Dunmore and several other Galway villages. Tower houses sprung up from Galway Bay in the west to Ballinasloe in the east and the most fertile land was taken from the native Irish. The O'Connor clan was driven east to Co. Roscommon, where they managed to partially maintain their strength. The 'Ferocious O'Flahertys', as they came to be known, were banished to the poor land of the

Athenry Castle (from *Irish Wonders* by D.R. McAnally Jr).

area west of Lough Corrib by the Norman invaders. They quickly supplanted the Keelys, who had ruled the area beforehand, and stamped their authority on the Connemara area, going on to build several castles. The Normans did attempt a couple of forays into Connemara, but soon realised it would be too difficult to supplant the Gaelic tribe and hardly worth their while for the poor-quality land. The O'Flahertys were thus left with the spoils. Connemara, a quarter of a million acres in size, was consequently largely untouched by Norman or English influence for hundreds of years afterwards and became a place apart from the rest of Galway. Galway City, finally a bastion of Norman rule, looked westwards with trepidation and later inscribed the plea 'From the ferocious O'Flahertys Good Lord Deliver Us' on the Western Gate.

Resistance against Normans remained in Galway, however, and on two occasions, including in 1247, Galway City was burned to the ground by the dispossessed Irish tribes. Three years earlier, the town of Tuam had also been razed. The Normans faced opposition to the south also and fought a battle against the O'Briens of Munster near Gort in the 1250s. Such opposition continued into the fourteenth century, when Edward Bruce, brother of Robert Bruce, King of Scotland, invaded the east coast of Ireland. The O'Connors, seeing their opportunity, joined Bruce's campaign and, with the assistance of several other local families, attacked Athenry in the Battle of Athenry in 1316. The Irish were again defeated and Felim O'Connor, their chief, was killed and had his head put on a spike overlooking the town. This defeat weakened the O'Connors, although they and the O'Flahertys would remain a thorn in the Normans' side for many years to come.

Despite this opposition, the Normans were determined to maintain their control of Galway and its environs. Eager to capitalise on the undoubted potential benefits of its location, they secured a borough charter for Galway City and began the building of fortified walls around it in 1272. The project took more than a century to complete but the location worked to the builders' advantage; the walls followed the natural defensive curve of a ridge, situated just to the north and east of the city, while the River Corrib offered further protection to the west. The de Burgos were the principal family in the town and gradually helped to establish it as a major economic centre, trading with far-flung nations such as Spain, France and Portugal. They also taxed sea trade in the area, using the considerable proceeds to finance the construction of fine buildings in Galway. St Nicholas' Church, an impressive building appropriately dedicated to the patron saint of seafarers, was erected in around 1320.

GALWAY AND THE TRIBES

By 1333, salmon and eel fisheries and a great harbour were among the main assets of Galway, and the economy of the city was booming, something that provided great benefits for the surrounding countryside as well. The east and west of the county provided much of the produce to be exported and the port of Galway acted as their means of delivering it to the wider world. The west of Ireland was closer to northern Spain and France, including the ports of Bordeaux and La Rochelle, than the ports on the east of Ireland were, giving it a strategic advantage and one that Galway exploited to the full. The town was also well supplied with fuel, with the abundant bogland and forestry in the surrounding area proving advantageous. The fast-flowing River Corrib was also among Galway's biggest advantages, acting as both a source of food and a natural means of powering the many mills that had sprung up in the area. It brought its own challenges as well, however, and it was not until the fourteenth century that a bridge was finally erected, connecting Galway City with the area west of the Corrib. Before this, travel was primarily done by boat. Lough Derg, in Co. Galway's southeast, was a similar challenge, although the town of Portumna already had a ferry crossing the Shannon at regular intervals at this point.

The Black Death of 1348 affected Galway, although its impact was less than in many other Irish areas. Nevertheless, it did reach the urban areas of the county through the ports and was likely to have been responsible for several thousand deaths, mainly of the Anglo-Normans, who were more likely to live in urban settings than the Gaelic Irish. Galway City certainly saw some inhabitants succumbing to the deadly disease, while Athenry was also said to have been badly affected. Regular expeditions departed Galway for continental ports throughout this period, despite the dangers, and succeeded in maintaining strong international connections, allowing the continued importation of exotic items and exclusive wines into Galway. Locally made products such as tallow and corn were exported on the return journeys and did a brisk continental trade.

Such trade led to Galway playing host to some notable visitors. Christopher Columbus is believed to have stopped into Galway in 1477 on one of his many expeditions and some sources suggest that a Galway man named William Harris was with him when he discovered the Americas in 1492. This economic activity also garnered much wealth for the upper classes of Galway, who came to be known as the Tribes of Galway. By the close of the fourteenth century, political and cultural life in Galway City, and by extension the county, had come to be dominated by fourteen important Anglo-Norman merchant families or Tribes. These were the Athy, Blake, Bodkin, Browne, D'Arcy, Deane, Font, Ffrench, Joyce, Kirwan, Lynch,

Lynch House, Galway (right) (from *Wanderings in Ireland* by Michael Myers Shoemaker).

Martin, Morris and Skerrit families. One of the most famous stories of Galway was said to have taken place in 1493 and was inextricably linked with one of the Tribes. In this year, it was stated that a young Spanish nobleman named Gomez was murdered by the son of James Lynch Fitzstephen, the mayor of Galway. In response, the mayor was said to have hanged his son publicly out a window in Market Street in the town to show that the law treated everyone equally. It has since been assumed by many that the verb 'to lynch' comes from this tale, something that in reality is unlikely to be true.

GALWAY'S POWER GROWS

The Galway Tribes, enriched by trading, were able to buy large tracts of land throughout rural Galway and the province of Connacht. The Anglo-Normans had become increasingly powerful in Ireland and comfortable in their adopted home, something that worried the English government. The Statutes of Kilkenny in 1366 were a futile attempt to ensure that Norman families, who had now been living in Ireland for several generations, remained English and did not conform to Irish norms of dress or speech. The statutes also listed the territories of Ireland considered loyal by the English – Galway was not on the list. The town of Galway was prospering economically despite its isolation from the other important towns of Ireland, such as Cork, Waterford and Dublin, all concentrated on the south and east coasts. It suffered a blow in 1473 when a large section of it was accidentally burned down. Undeterred, this ultimately provided Galwegians with the impetus to replace many of the more dilapidated old wooden buildings with more modern constructions.

Galway's denizens, usually members of one of the afore-mentioned Tribes, regularly rose to national prominence and Galway was finally granted city status in 1484. A later detailed and ornate map of Galway City shows us what the city was like in its heyday, indicating that the well-built, intricate street patterns of the time, which remain largely the same today, used the natural geography of the area to great effect to enclose and protect its 21 acres. Within the newly formed city of Galway, most inhabitants remained English in language and outlook.

The county was very different. By the fifteenth and sixteenth centuries, most of those living outside the city walls had become more Irish than the Irish themselves, while loyalty to the Crown had waned. The de Burgos had once been the most powerful Norman family in Galway but by the fifteenth century they had become Gaelicised. Ultimately, they became known as the Burkes, and owned much of the land of east Galway. The Burkes were eventually ostracised by the Tribes of Galway due to their close relationship with the native Irish and were largely frozen out of power in the city.

On 19 August 1504, the Burke clan fought the Battle of Knockdoe near Claregalway against the Earl of Kildare. Ulick Burke had apparently being having an affair with the wife of Tadhg O'Kelly, an ally of the Earl of Kildare, and had

Grace O'Malley (from *Stories and Legends of Travel and History* by Grace Greenwood).

also commandeered O'Kelly's land near Ballinasloe. The earl, from the Pale and fiercely loyal to the English Crown, decided to strike and attack the Burkes, who were no longer living under the king's writ. It was a bloody battle and the earl's army eventually won out and went on to attack several of the Burkes' castles throughout Co. Galway. The defeat was a victory for British power in Ireland and was widely known as 'the Death of Gaelic Ireland'.

Connemara was another area that largely ignored English law. Piracy was common on its rocky shores in the sixteenth century, much of it spearheaded by a woman named Grace O'Malley. She spent much of her life in County Galway, despite being born in neighbouring Co. Mayo on Clare Island in 1530. Nicknamed *Gráinne Mhaol* (Bald Grace) after cutting her own hair short as a young child in order to be able to look like a boy and join her father's seafaring expeditions, Grace proved herself an able sailor and trav-elled all over Europe. At the age of 16, she married Donal of the neighbouring O'Flaherty tribe, which had previously been sworn enemies of the O'Malleys, a union that further added to her wealth and notoriety. When her father died, she assumed control of his whole fleet, which was able to control much of Ireland's west coast. She sailed to many countries, trading all sorts of goods. Many of the tactics used to gain control of the sea were not strictly legal and Grace earned another nickname: the Pirate Queen. Grace moved to her husband's home at Bunowen Castle, near Ballyconneely in Co. Galway, in the late 1540s and lived there with Donal and the pair's three children until her hus-band was killed in battle in 1565. After this, Grace married another powerful chieftain, Richard Bourke.

Grace continued to prosper, dividing her time between the sea and several castles, including at Bunowen and Renvyle in Co. Galway. She fought many battles against neighbouring tribes, especially the Joyces, and proved a fierce opponent. The west of Ireland had always proven difficult to control from an English perspective, largely due to the O'Malleys, and presidents of the provinces were appointed from 1569 onwards in an attempt to make maintaining control easier. It was at this point that the counties of Connacht were shired to make them easier to manage – Galway was one of five counties drawn up in the west, along with Mayo, Sligo, Leitrim and Roscommon. Together, they comprised the province of Connacht. Richard Bingham was appointed president in 1584 and was nicknamed 'the Flail of Connacht' due to his violent methods of controlling the region. At one session in Galway in 1586, he put seventy people to death. He was also a sworn enemy of *Gráinne Mhaol*. She requested and was granted a meeting with Queen Elizabeth I to complain about his arrest of her family members. The queen must have been impressed by her visitor as she agreed to return many of Grace's titles and some of her land. Grace continued her life at sea until an old age, before she died in 1603. From this point on, the Crown would find it a little easier to control the seas around Co. Galway.

Queen Elizabeth I
(Dover Publications).

3

REFORMATION AND PLANTATION IN GALWAY

THE REFORMATION IN GALWAY

The Reformation originated in Germany in 1517 when Martin Luther began to agitate against the corruption of the Catholic Church and a new religion, Protestantism, was born shortly afterwards. This movement quickly spread to England. Henry VIII, after initially reaffirming his faith in Catholicism, later decided to embrace Protestantism after being refused permission to obtain a divorce from the Catholic Church. There had been a parliament in place in Ireland since shortly after the coming of the Normans, although only the elite could vote and its influence was negligible, especially in the west. The members of the Irish parliament passed the Act of Supremacy in 1537, which pledged allegiance to Henry VIII and his new religion. This kickstarted efforts to suppress Catholicism in Ireland, something that would be the catalyst for centuries of intermittent sectarian strife on the island. Many of the Galway Tribes converted to Protestantism in the decades afterwards. Outside the city, however, Gaelic and Catholic culture continued to prevail.

The English thus remained unconvinced of Ireland's loyalty and a failed rebellion in the 1530s led by Silken Thomas of Kildare further convinced them that action need to be taken to ensure loyalty. They enacted two controversial policies. Firstly, they adopted surrender and regrant, a policy under which the landowners of Ireland were forced to give up their land. They were then regranted it on the condition that they agreed to abide by the laws of the Crown. The second policy was plantation of British people on to the island of Ireland. In 1556, the counties of Laois and Offaly, the latter directly to Galway's east, were planted. Gaelic Irish land was seized and given to the planters. Munster would follow later in the century. However, there were too few planters and they ended up living in isolated country regions with little protection, leading to a constant battle to hold onto their land. The Irish had little control of their own affairs officially, and the west, being overwhelmingly rural and dominated by Gaelic tribes, was particularly poorly represented. A parliament in Dublin in 1560, for example, was composed of seventy-six members. Fifty of these were from the province of Leinster. The whole province of Connacht had only two boroughs entitled to send representatives, Galway and Athenry, giving Galway little say in the laws under which they would live.

The Spanish Armada

Another important event in sixteenth-century Galway was the Spanish Armada of 1588. Relations between Catholic Spain and Protestant England had become strained, with King Philip of Spain believing that he had a claim to the English throne. In 1587, with Francis Drake leading an attack on the Spanish territory of Cadiz, Spain opted for all-out war on their enemies. In May 1588, nearly 30,000 men and more than 130 ships set off from Spain for England with the express intention of overthrowing Queen Elizabeth I. The huge force planned to enter the English Channel, provoke an English response, and by force of numbers defeat any ships that came their way. The attack did not go as planned and English fireships managed to destroy several vessels at the centre of the Spanish fleet, leaving their cohesive plan in tatters and inadvertently ensuring that Galway would play a role in the ensuing carnage that befell the defeated army.

The beleaguered Spanish decided to sail north around Scotland, hoping to then be able to round Ireland and return to their home country. Inclement weather intervened and the ships were driven off course. Many were shipwrecked, some at Antrim and on the north coast and others off Sligo. Several would find a watery grave off the coast of Co. Galway. One vessel, with fifty-eight crewmen, foundered off the coast of Carna and today gives its name to *Duarlaing na Spáinneach* – the Spaniard's Beach. Eighty-eight others came ashore near Barna. The Elizabethan government had given orders not to spare any Spanish soldier who managed to make it onshore at Galway. The president of Connacht, Richard Bingham, took the queen at her word and executed more than 1,000 survivors who made it to shore. Three hundred of the crew of a ship that foundered in Galway Bay were taken to St Augustine's Church on a hill above Galway City and beheaded. It is believed that a tiny number made their way to safety and were sheltered by the people of South Connemara, where they lived out their days. Over the centuries Galway has often been said to have a Spanish influence, whether through this event or as a result of its trade over centuries with the country. As late as 1904, M.F. Mansfield stated:

One notes as he strolls through the Galway market, where the
women are selling fish, in their complexions, their dark hair and
eyes, their high cheek-bones, and their carriage, – in the *mantilla*-
like way in which they wear their shawls, and in the brilliant
colours of their costumes, they bear a striking resemblance to the
fisherwomen of Cadiz and Malaga. The men are even more strik-
ingly Spanish.[3]

As the 1590s dawned, more plantations were planned for
Ireland. Although Galway remained unplanted, there was
a realisation that any county could be chosen for a massive influx of English settlers, and in the 1590s Ulster native
Red Hugh O'Donnell and his army challenged the planters
and English authority, forming a large army and sacking
many of the most important Norman towns on the island.
Their campaign was successful at first and they made it as
far as Connacht, where they attacked Norman strongholds
and burned much of the eastern suburbs of Galway City.
The emboldened Gaelic Irish also attacked the Norman
stronghold of Athenry in 1596 and burned the town to the
ground, defacing its coat of arms. Among O'Donnell's most
important allies in Galway were the Clanricarde Burkes,
who were descendants of the de Burgos, once the foremost
Norman tribe in Galway. Red Hugh's rebellion was eventually crushed when his army and their Spanish allies were
defeated at the Battle of Kinsale in 1601. Red Hugh went
to Spain to seek further support, where he died suddenly
the following year. He had been in the company of James
Blake, a Galway man, and there were rumours that Blake
had been paid by the English to administer poison to their
deadly foe. In 1607, the O'Donnell family, in conjunction
with their allies the O'Neills, who had ruled most of Ulster,

3   Mansfield, M.F. & B.M. (1904), *Romantic Ireland*, p.134.

left Ireland in what became known as the 'Flight of the Earls'. They were never to return and Ulster was planted in the following decades with thousands of English and Scottish families.

THE CROMWELLIAN PLANTATIONS

At the beginning of the seventeenth century, Galway was only the eleventh largest town in Ireland. Nevertheless, it had the second strongest walled fortifications of any Irish town, abundant natural resources and a well-built harbour. Oliver St John said of it in 1614:

> It is small but has fair and stately buildings, the fronts of the houses are all hewed stone, garnished with fair battlements. The merchants are rich and great adventurers at sea. They keep good hospitality and are kind to strangers.[4]

Although Galway City would go on to become Galway's biggest and most important urban area, at this point there were several rivals for that crown. Athenry was an impressive settlement built around the Norman castle with a bustling market, and the Dominican priory in the town was briefly recognised as a university. Loughrea was the location of the county gaol since 1585 and the County Assizes two decades later. Tuam had been declining in importance since the thirteenth century, but was revitalised in 1613 when it received a royal charter that allowed it to send two representatives to parliament along with Athenry and Galway. Ballinasloe, too, was a town on the up, and by the 1630s the Trench family had come to the area and played

4   St John, O. (1614), *A Description of Connaught*, p.13.

an important role in building up the town on the River Suck as an industrial and market town for the district.

Any hopes for continued prosperity for the towns of Galway would be dashed by outside events, however. In 1641, a rebellion against English law in Ireland began, amidst widespread dissatisfaction and rumours that more counties, including Galway, were to be planted. The rebellion was largely confined to Ulster and many of the English and Scottish planters were targeted, several thousand being killed. England too was in turmoil, a civil war raging between the supporters of the King of England, Charles I, and parliamentarians under Oliver Cromwell, many of whom were strict Protestants wishing to depose the monarch. Most Irish Catholics, both Normans and native Irish, backed the king at the Confederation of Kilkenny. They agreed to help the royal war effort in return for concessions to Catholics. Unfortunately for them, Cromwell's forces were victorious after the lengthy conflict and Charles I was beheaded in 1649, apparently at the hands of a Galway native named Deane.

Cromwell thus won power and quickly set his eyes on Ireland, arriving on Irish shores in 1649 with 12,000 battle-hardened soldiers. Cromwell had a deep hatred for Irish Catholics, motivated by their aiding of the king and the attacks on Protestant settlers in 1641, and he was keen to overrun the island and parcel out its land as payment to his soldiers. His army laid siege to the country, massacring thousands and destroying towns such as Drogheda and Wexford. When the puritan forces finally reached Galway in 1651, the town refused to surrender and its advantageous location between the Atlantic Ocean and Lough Corrib allowed it to hold out for ten months. Its thick stone walls and fourteen defensive towers also proved adept at keeping invaders out, but the town was blockaded from receiving any supplies. Eventually, starvation and disease forced the people to surrender in May 1652. The survivors were dealt with severely. Many Galway people were killed outright, while others were sent as slaves to work on plantations in the West Indies.

Connemara was next to face the horrors of the New Model Army. The O'Flaherty clan had run the area as their own fiefdom since the arrival of the Normans 400 years before. Led by Edmond O'Flaherty, they refused to submit to Cromwell's rule. The army probed deep into the mountainous region, capturing and killing many of the natives, including Edmond himself. Once the final outpost, Inishbofin Island, surrendered in 1653, all residents of Connemara were ordered to leave their homes and move inland at least 3 miles from the sea to prevent smuggling or communicating with enemy mariners.

With Ireland subjugated, almost all good-quality land was confiscated, the owners being given the choice of being killed or migrating to the western province. 'To Hell or to Connacht' was the cry to all disloyal Irish landowners. Charles Coote, an English officer, was put in charge of Connacht, which he ruled from his base in Galway City. Even in Connacht, the best land was awarded to Cromwellian settlers, many of whom sold up and returned to England, leaving the settlers who remained with huge tracts. Galway City, a centre of commerce and industry, as well as a military stronghold, was considered strategically vital and it was placed in the hands of those whom the Cromwellian regime felt they could trust. Many of the former occupants were expelled, their fine townhouses being taken by these former soldiers.

LIFE AFTER CROMWELL

Amongst the Cromwellian settlers were the Eyre family from Wiltshire, who went on to become one of Galway's premier families. John and Edward Eyre were given tens of thousands of acres between them in east Galway and they purchased even more in the following years. Edward became mayor of Galway, as did several of the family's descendants. Eyre Square in the city, as well as the village of Eyrecourt, are named after the family. A smattering of Catholic landowners from superior lands in the east were also exiled to Galway as punishment. Any landowner who disobeyed and attempted to remain east of the Shannon faced severe penalties, including banishment or death. Just one example of many was Richard Nugent, the Earl of Westmeath, who was a leading royalist fighting against Cromwell. He was punished by the parliamentarians by being stripped of his rich pastureland in Leinster and transplanted to Renvyle in north-west Connemara, where he was given 14,000 acres of poor mountainous land. It is believed he never even visited his new estate, selling it off in 1680.

Protestants now owned most of the land of Ireland and a transplantation of poorer Catholic people, many from Ulster, occurred. The defeated and deflated families were forced to march to Connacht, including Galway, and take up tenancies on the poorer land there. Cromwell was a hater of Catholicism and his army killed and banished priests and destroyed churches in the 1650s. To make matters worse, these events were followed by a famine and fever that ravaged Galway and the country at large, and it is believed that more than a fifth of the Irish population died in the decade between 1642 and 1652.

A map of Ireland illustrating the Cromwellian Settlement. Galway is one of just three counties 'assigned to Irish' (from *Ireland under the Stuarts* by Bagwell).

The English monarchy was restored in 1660 after Cromwell's death. Most of the Anglo-Norman families were granted compensatory land as a reward for their loyalty, some receiving back what had been taken from them, although they were never again to wield the power that had been theirs for centuries. The Gaelic Irish families, such as the O'Flahertys, were given nothing, despite having also supported the king. To make matters worse, the Penal Laws were introduced over the coming decade. These sectarian laws intensified the oppression of Catholics and forbade them from receiving an education, owning expensive property or standing for parliament.

Before the 1640s, Galway had been one of Ireland's economic success stories and as late as 1657 the Privy Council was stating: 'That as for the commerce it had with Spain, the Straits and the West Indies, it is not inferior to any port in the three countries, London excepted.' The coming decades saw it much reduced from its former opulence, however. The Cromwellian colonists had assumed control of the city and were suspicious of the strongly Catholic population that had proven able to withstand their lengthy siege. Far from co-operating with the natives and capitalising on their knowledge of foreign lands and merchant connections honed from trade and travel over centuries, the authorities stripped many Catholics of their land and titles and barred them from becoming members of the Corporation. Unsurprisingly, trade declined markedly over the following decades and the formerly busy harbour became a shadow of its former self.

Meanwhile, trade from Europe to other continents was increasing steadily and the size of vessels and transactions was equally expanding. The location of the southern ports of Waterford and Cork benefitted from the passing British trade to the colonies, most of which travelled south of

Ireland. Meanwhile, Limerick and Sligo on the west coast were closer to mainland England and Scotland respectively, leaving Galway isolated. Galway's harbour was also shallow and less suitable for modern boats, which had grown ever larger. This affected the entire county. The rural areas had long become accustomed to their produce being bought at the ports and exported overseas. Overland trade also began to rival sea trade in Ireland at the time, Dublin merchants capitalising with an improved distribution network to outlying towns. The lack of an easily traversable road from Galway to Dublin was thus proving to be an issue, a postal system only being established in Galway in 1653, several years after other port towns. The rural areas of Galway, meanwhile, were even more isolated and the areas furthest from the Galway to Dublin road were isolated from the economic life of the country. John Dunton visited Galway in 1698, and he described the road from Athenry to the city, despite it being one of the busiest highways in the west, as 'little more than sheep walks for two miles and all the rest of the way rocky and barren'.

THE WAR OF THE TWO KINGS

The War of the Two Kings was the next violent episode in Irish history and the bloodiest battle of the conflict occurred on Galway soil, just outside the small village of Aughrim in the east of the county. The seeds of war were sown when King James II ascended to the English throne in 1685. James was a Catholic, something that alarmed the Protestant parliament of England. Although James II was the rightful heir to the crown of England, politicians instead invited the Dutch Protestant king, William of Orange, who was married to James' daughter Mary, to challenge for the

James II in battle (from *A Popular History of England* by M. Guizot).

English throne with their support. He did so, successfully usurping James in the Glorious Revolution of 1688. James went into exile and the Irish, overwhelmingly Catholic and mistreated by the Penal Laws, quickly backed the Catholic monarch who they hoped would regrant them their land. By this point, only 20 per cent of Irish land was in Catholic hands, even though they made up the vast majority of the population. The Protestant settlers of Ulster were sympathetic to their co-religionist William, however. The War of the Two Kings was the result and although much of the war would take place on Irish soil, Holland, France, and other European powers took a great interest in this significant conflict, France having allied themselves with James and Holland with William.

There was a major engagement in Co. Meath, the Battle of the Boyne on 12 July 1690, which was won by William's forces. The Williamites crossed the River Shannon in the spring of 1691 and managed to capture the strategic town of Athlone after a lengthy siege on 30 June. Two weeks later, the two sides faced off on 12 July 1691 at Aughrim, Co. Galway. James' supporters, the Jacobites, had positioned themselves on a small hill, giving them a positional advantage in the flat east Galway countryside. This necessitated their enemies attacking uphill, through a bog, in misty conditions. The Jacobite force looked to be routing their opponents until their general, a Frenchman named Saint Ruthe, was killed by a cannonball. He was later buried in Loughrea. This loss sucked the life out of the Jacobites and their defences quickly began to fall apart. They were pushed back down the hill, where many turned and fled, others being killed by the Williamite cavalry. Many of their most experienced officers were among the casualties. It is believed that upwards of 40,000 soldiers fought in the epic battle and that 8,000 people were killed, surely making it the bloodiest day in Galway's history.

A peace treaty was ultimately signed between the two sides. The Treaty of Limerick promised freedom of religion and the right of Catholics to own property. The treaty

Site of the Battle of Aughrim (from *An Illustrated History of Ireland* by Mary Frances Cusack).

was broken by the Protestant elite before the ink was dry. After the Treaty of Limerick, the Dublin parliament, which still only permitted Protestants as members, voted in even more draconian Penal Laws. Most Catholic priests were banished and the building of Catholic churches banned. Worship was severely curtailed and Catholics were forced to attend Mass in secret at 'Mass rocks' on hills around the country. There are many of these to be found in Galway, at Shantalla, Barna and Esker. Members of the Catholic religion were also prohibited from voting, owning a weapon or buying land from a Protestant. Moreover, their children were barred from attending school. Many Catholic parents were anxious that their children should receive an education, however, and hedge schools with unofficial schoolmasters flourished throughout the county over the next century. Woodford, for example, was known to have several hedge schools in fields and mountains in the area. Five hedge schools also existed in Ardrahan as late as 1835, including one in the village church where a teacher named Patrick Connolly taught on a salary of £10 a year. These hedge schools were small establishments in which a teacher taught reading, writing and arithmetic skills to pupils in return for a small fee, and they succeeded in keeping the flame of education alight throughout Galway. Irish history and culture were also kept alive in these schools.

LIFE IN EIGHTEENTH-CENTURY GALWAY

The Popery Act of 1703 further marginalised Galway members of the Catholic faith, the bill containing clauses allowing Catholics who already resided in the town to remain there only if they gave a bond of loyalty to the Crown. Under these circumstances, converting to

Protestantism had its benefits and many wealthy Catholics changed their religion in an attempt to hold on to their land. This was not universal, however. Several branches of the Blake family, one of the Tribes of Galway, converted to the established church, while others stayed true to the faith of their fathers. Connemara remained largely aloof of these developments and was still under the control of the O'Flahertys. The Joyce clan also wielded much power since their arrival in the region in the thirteenth century, originally as an English colony. They quickly adopted the Irish language and customs, and members of the family were so numerous in north Connemara between Lough Mask and Lough Corrib that the area came to be known as Joyce Country. A young Frenchman named De Lotocnaye visited Galway in the eighteenth century. Connemara was such a distinct place that he was warned not to enter it. He wrote:

> Connemara is less known than the islands of the Pacific Ocean … Persons [in Galway] from whom I asked information begged me not to visit such a barbarous country, where I should not find a dry stone to sit down on, and where the few inhabitants were as barbarous as the Iroquois.[5]

The Frenchman entered the region nonetheless, even reaching the far western coast where few outsiders had travelled. He found the people hospitable. The isolation meant that Connemara remained a haven for smugglers and law and order of the British variety was largely unknown. George O'Malley was a renowned smuggler who was said to have sailed all over Europe and brought exotic goods home to Connemara without paying excise. Other places closer to Galway City also had a history of smuggling – Oranmore

5   Da Lotocnaye, C. (1797), *A Frenchman's Walk Through Ireland*, p.151.

was one coastal village where many people entered by sea and traded stealthily, thus avoiding the high government taxes.

Life was not all doom and gloom in eighteenth-century Galway. Traditional music and dance had been popular since Celtic times and remained important in Galway, while instruments such as the uilleann pipes, flute and harp were played at feasts, patterns and other celebrations. Seanchaí, or travelling storytellers, were another very important form of entertainment in Irish life at the time and poets were highly respected. One of the most famous poets was Anthony Raftery. He was blind, yet was able to travel all over the west of Ireland, visiting houses to play music and recite poems he had written. People would come from far and wide to listen to him and his stories and poetry, and he spent much of his later life in and around Loughrea, where he is believed to have died. Due to his blindness, Raftery never wrote down his compositions. Fortunately, however, others did and they have been recorded and remain popular to this day. An annual festival, Féile Raifteirí, is held in the town in his honour, while Craughwell village has a statue commemorating him.

The following pre-Famine poem is an ode to the people of the west of Ireland, written from the perspective of a wandering Galway musician and storyteller:

Green hills of the west, where I carolled along,
In the Mayday of life with my harp and my song;
Though the winter of time o'er my spirit hath rolled,
And the breast of the minstrel is weary and cold.

Though no more by those famous old haunts shall I stray,
Once the themes of my song, and the guides of my way;
That each had its story, and a true-hearted friend,
Before I forget ye, life's journey shall end!

I had tales for the hamlet, and news for the hall,
And the tune of old times, ever welcome to all,
The praise of thy glory, dear land of the west;
But thy praises are still, and thy kind bosoms rest!

My blessing rest with you, dear friends, though no more
Shall the poor and the weary rejoice at your door;
Though like stars to your homes I have seen you depart,
Still ye live, O ye live, in each vein of my heart.[6]

LIFE AS A TENANT IN CO. GALWAY

Although the Penal Laws were onerous on the people of Galway, some of the county's gentry remained Catholic, particularly in the east of the county, and the dreaded laws were not fully implemented against them. The landlords, Catholic or Protestant, lived in what was termed 'the big house' and rented out parcels of land to their tenants. Some of the Galway landlords were the Cromwellian planters or their descendants, while other estates had been restored to the Anglo-Normans elites, often called the Old English. The vast majority of the population were tenants, however, and it was a very difficult time to be a poor Catholic farmer in Galway. Large families living on tiny plots of land was the norm. Having ten to twelve children was not uncommon, although child mortality rates were exceptionally high. Houses were often made of perishable material and had a thatched roof, rendering them damp, cold and wholly unsuited to Galway's wet and windy climate. Barns and outhouses were largely unknown and animals, such as the cow, were so important to the family's prospects that they were

6 'The Minstrel's Walk', printed in the *Irish Penny Journal*, 2 January 1841.

regularly allowed to share living quarters with the family in the depths of winter. Fishing was an important industry in coastal regions but was a precarious and dangerous existence with rudimentary equipment. Malnourishment, disease and early death were a huge part of life and a father often subdivided his farm among several of his children, leading to ever-smaller farm sizes.

The people had one food that was both a blessing and a curse – the potato. It had become the staple food of the poor by 1700, having been introduced to Ireland in 1589 from the Americas by Walter Raleigh. The vegetable soon became popular as it did not require much soil or sunlight to grow and was an easy way for Irish families to feed themselves. This was even more the case in western counties such as Galway, particularly in Connemara where the soil was rocky and barren. The abundance of the potato saw the population rise exponentially, more than doubling between 1700, when it was just over 2 million, and 1800, when it had climbed to 5 million. Numerous famines occurred in that time frame when bad weather or disease affected the potato harvest, causing the price of other food, such as grain, to skyrocket. The famine of 1740–41 was particularly disastrous. It came about after three consecutive freezing winters and it is believed that one fifth of the population may have died from starvation and disease as a result.

There was unrest in Galway, particularly among poorer Catholics who were deeply unhappy with their status as second-class citizens and with the terrible conditions in which they were forced to live. The continued payment of tithes, a tax on Catholics and other religions to pay for the upkeep of the established Church, was also deeply resented. Food riots occurred in the county on a regular basis in the eighteenth century. These usually involved starving, desperate crowds attacking local potato stores or mills in which oatmeal was stored to try to distribute the contents. Secret societies known variously as the Ribbonmen, the Whiteboys and the Terry Alts were also set up and operated in the county agitating for tenants' rights. At this time, there was an increase of land used for grazing and beef cattle, in part because pasture land was exempt from tithes, incentivising landlords to force smaller tenants off the land. These secret societies sent threatening letters, and in more extreme cases used arson and violence against animals and people to try and force change.

In the wake of this unrest, Ireland was again granted its own parliament in Dublin in 1782 but this did little to assuage Catholics. Grattan's parliament, as it was known, did not allow Catholics to partake, although many members did proclaim their support for Catholic Emancipation. Sectarianism remained a problem and although there were instances of it in Galway, violence between the communities was most common in Ulster, where the numbers of Protestants and Catholics were more evenly distributed. In the winter of 1795, after an armed confrontation between the two groups occurred in Co. Armagh, the victorious Protestants forcibly expelled thousands of Catholics, who were forced to leave carrying only what they could on their back in freezing conditions. Many came as far as Co. Galway, particularly to the estate of Richard Martin in Connemara, who was moved by the refugees' plight. One newspaper report from 1796 stated that he gave asylum to approximately 'a thousand miserable souls on his estate, all peaceable, inoffensive and living by the labour of their hands'. Martin gave each family free rent for several years, only requiring them to begin payment when they had built their house and begun tilling their land. Many settled in the townland of Coogla, near Roundstone. Coogla's name comes from the Irish *Cuige Uladh* – the province of Ulster.

Other 'Ultachs', as they were termed, came to the estate of Thomas Burke at Marble Hill, near Woodford, and worked hard to integrate into the local community. It was said that they built strong stone houses and introduced linen weaving to the area.

4

THE 1798 REBELLION AND THE DAWN OF THE NINETEENTH CENTURY

THE 1798 REBELLION

Ireland was not immune to outside influences and the revolutions in America and France at the end of the eighteenth century captured the public imagination to such an extent that it inspired an Irish revolution in 1798. Theobald Wolfe Tone was one of its main instigators. Tone was a Dublin-born Protestant who had lived in Galway in 1783 for a year when he worked as a tutor for the family of the MP Richard Martin, often known as 'Humanity Dick' due to his love of animals and his pivotal role in the founding of the Royal Society of the Prevention of Cruelty to Animals (RSPCA). The Martins, although Protestants and extensive landowners themselves, were popular with the Catholics of Galway and were keenly aware of the injustices faced by them in the form of the Penal Laws. Martin wanted to see parliamentary reform and more Irish influence on their own affairs. Catholics were also regular visitors to the Martin home, something that Tone had not been familiar with in his youth.

Wolfe Tone (from *The Story of Ireland* by Emily Lawless).

This open attitude to Catholics had a profound effect on Wolfe Tone and it would come to shape his attitude and ultimately change the course of Irish history. In 1791, Tone helped to found the United Irishmen, which worked to persuade the working classes from both Catholic and Protestant communities that they could find common cause with one another in their grievances. He also believed that Ireland should be free and only then would Catholics and Presbyterians be given freedoms denied to them by the established elite. In May 1798, a rebellion broke out with thousands of rebels catching the British by surprise. After some early victories, particularly in Co. Wexford, the United Irishmen were crushed when reinforcements from Britain were drafted in and tactics such as half-hanging, pitchcapping and mass execution were used to elicit surrender from the poorly armed rebels.

Galway was not at the centre of this revolution, which was primarily based in the south-east, as well as in the northern counties of Antrim and Down. In fact, the government considered Galway one of the best-behaved parts of Ireland. Nevertheless, guns were seized in Loughrea by a local magistrate, who dumped them in a local lake lest they be used against the authorities. A small number of insurgents in the same area were also arrested. The French did consider landing a force in Co. Galway to help the rebels but ultimately came on shore in neighbouring Mayo in August

1798, fighting a famous battle at Castlebar against British forces. The rebellion was quickly suppressed in the west nevertheless, and the mountains of Connemara became home to several 1798 fugitives from British law, including Mayo native Fr Myles Prendergast, who survived in the mountains with the help of the locals until his death in 1842.

The British showed no mercy to Irish soldiers in 1798 and wished to ensure that no such uprising would occur again. William Pitt, the British prime minister, managed to persuade the Irish parliament to sanction its own abolishment and in 1800 passed the Act of Union that disestablished the Irish parliament and joined Ireland with England, Wales and Scotland in the United Kingdom. A further attempted revolution in 1803 led by Robert Emmet was also concentrated in Dublin and passed by in Galway with a whimper. Emmet himself was beheaded for his part. The Catholic majority were cowed by these events but violence against the unfair circumstances in which they were forced to live was never far away. The British administration feared that Irish rebels might once again collude with the French and organise a seabound invasion. For this reason, more than fifty Martello towers were built around the coast to watch for French vessels. There are a number of these in Co. Galway, including at Rossaveel in Connemara and Aughinish on the border with Co. Clare. To complement these coastal fortifications, a number of inland watchtowers were constructed on the River Shannon, including at Meelick, Co. Galway.

DEVELOPMENT IN GALWAY

In the face of many economic challenges, Galway saw some developments and some measure of urbanisation in the early part of the nineteenth century. Despite its huge expanse, Connemara had no town to speak of until 1812, when John D'Arcy founded one at Clifden. Located at Ardbear Bay in an important maritime location, it was one of the most westerly towns in Ireland and eventually helped to integrate Connemara and Galway after a traversable road between the two was built in the 1830s. Roundstone was also built nearby by engineer Alexander Nimmo in the following decade, as he travelled around the west designing bridges and roads. Loughrea had been a significant settlement for centuries and, in 1818, it was described by T. Walford as:

> A well-built village, and will receive the tourist in exploring the eastern district as a central station. See the fine lake; pleasing prospects; ruins of the old Castle of the De Burghs and various castle ruins in the vicinity.[7]

Ballinasloe was home to a flour mill and three oatmeal mills on the River Suck as well as several factories, two breweries, a large bacon-curing establishment and a felt hat manufacturer. Gort, too, was a product of the early nineteenth century, having been built in 1806 and enlarged in 1836. It gained a reputation as a good market town with dozens of businesses supplying the surrounding community including hatters, wheelwrights, chandlers, shoemakers, weavers, solicitors, grocers and at one point more than thirty public houses. The establishment of a linen market at Ballygar crossroads in north-east Galway in 1818 led to a town quickly springing up around it, while Glenamaddy began to develop in the 1820s when a regular market servicing the surrounding area began to attract investment.

---

7   Walford, T. (1818), *The Scientific Tourist through Ireland*, p.38.

Tuam remained a significant population centre, although Daniel Beaufort, an English rector, visited the town in the late eighteenth century and was less impressed. He stated that:

> Much dirt is thrown out the window and the streets are perfectly dark. Many people here collect dirt into the courts of houses where they make a heap until the season for putting it out. There is therefore frequent occasion for holding one's nose.[8]

As for Galway City in the early nineteenth century, visitors might remark on the fine buildings and evidence of past glories but it was clearly a faded grandeur of a Galway that had seen better days. Hardiman lamented that the city, once the second most important harbour in Ireland, was by 1820 surpassed by Limerick and Waterford and its neglected streets, the 'worst-paved in this country', were now regularly impassable with filth and water. Signs of the potential of the natural resources in the Galway area were still to be found, however. There were twenty flour mills using the power of the River Corrib, with wheat being grown widely in the hinterland. There were woollen mills and several distilleries as well, including Persse's Brewery, which manufactured porter at Newcastle.

HARDSHIP IN THE WEST

Lough Corrib, and the river that takes its name from it, were also important transport routes in the early eighteenth century and much of Galway's travel and commercial activity occurred on the waterway. Fishing was also an important means of earning a livelihood, both at sea and on inland

---

8 Beaufort, S. (1787), *Journal of Samuel Beaufort – Tuam.*

waterways. Basking shark was hunted for its oil, while cod, ling and herring were among the fish sought in Galway Bay. Shellfish and lobsters were also abundant. Rivers and lakes could also be important sources of food and Ballynahinch had one of Ireland's foremost salmon fisheries. Sadly, the boats used in these activities were of a rudimentary nature at the time and there were many water-based fatalities in Galway. Lough Corrib played host to one of the county's worst tragedies on 4 September 1828. That morning, some thirty-one people boarded an old boat at Annaghdown Pier to travel the 8 miles to a fair at Galway City. There were also several sheep and other goods for sale on the boat. The old vessel struggled to take the weight and near Menlo a sheep was said to have put its hoof through a plank, causing water to rush in. At least nineteen people were drowned, despite the heroic rescue efforts of several passengers. The tragedy is commemorated in Raftery's Poem 'Anach Cuan', and there is a memorial to the victims at Annaghdown Pier.

Life in the early nineteenth century was arduous for city and rural dwellers alike and life expectancy remained low, most people unlikely to see their fortieth birthday. Malnourishment and diseases of all sorts were common. In 1832 alone, 295 men died of cholera in Galway City. The Scottish engineer Alexander Nimmo was well acquainted with the people of Galway and described them as being in 'almost the lowest possible state of existence, their cabins are in the most miserable conditions and the food is potatoes with water very often without anything else'. He added that they frequently begged him on their knees to give them some employment.

It is therefore unsurprising that petty crime was common, particularly minor thefts, and a group called the Galway Watchmen, forerunners of the police, was set up to deter would-be criminals in the 1820s. Lawmakers had little sympathy for those desperate enough to commit crimes, however.

Between the years 1791 and 1853, penal transportation to the underpopulated British colony of Australia was a common punishment in Ireland for many misdemeanours, some highly innocuous. Some 26,500 Irishmen and women were among the unfortunate souls forced to make the journey to the other side of the world in a convict ship in those sixty years, many from Galway. Execution was also regularly used as a punishment for various crimes. In 1819 and 1820, several Galway men were executed for offences such as breaking into houses and administering illegal oaths. Among the dead was Anthony Daly, a member of the secret society The Ribbonmen in the Craughwell area. Daly was hanged at Seefin Hill, overlooking the spot where several men had attempted to shoot landlord James Hardiman Burke. Transportation was also a common punishment for being a member of a secret society – twenty-six Galway men, for example, were banished to Australia on the ship *Eliza* in May 1832.

Thomas Laffey was one Galway man who was transported to Australia for what today reads like a very minor offence. The 30-year-old of Ballinakill was indicted for having, on 17 January 1838, stolen four sheep, the property of Thomas Coyne near Clifden. Coyne had been shown wool by the police seventeen days later that he believed matched that of his stolen sheep. Laffey allegedly admitted his guilt to the police and was found guilty and sentenced to a very harsh seven years' transportation, effectively a life sentence in Australia due

Daniel O'Connell (from *The History of Ireland* by John F. Finerty).

to the practical impossibility of returning to Ireland at that time. In response to the sentence, Laffey told the court that he did not care if they had him executed. It appears Laffey duly arrived to Australia the following year and after seven years working under a master named Morgan received his certificate of freedom. What became of him afterwards is unknown.

THE MOVEMENT FOR REPEAL

Daniel O'Connell was one man who believed Irish men and women would have a better chance of a prosperous life in a just society under an Irish parliament. The solicitor was a Catholic and believed that a mass movement of the Irish, committed to non-violent means, could secure Catholic Emancipation. This was much desired by the people of Galway, although as the eighteenth century wore on the authorities had increasingly turned a blind eye to the Penal Laws. In fact, there were already more than 100 places of Catholic worship in Co. Galway, while most businessmen and landlords in the town of Loughrea were of the Catholic faith even before Catholic Emancipation was finally passed in 1829. Tuam had a Catholic church in the town as early as 1783 and Catholics were largely allowed to worship without harassment. Nevertheless, there was much celebration in Galway on the passing of Catholic Emancipation.

After Emancipation had been achieved, O'Connell's next aim was the repeal of the Act of Union and the foundation of a parliament in Dublin. Renowned for his oration skills, he held 'Monster Meetings' all over the country to show the British government the level of support the idea of repealing the Act of Union had among ordinary people. In a time before motorised transport of any kind, people walked for miles to listen to the charismatic leader. He spoke in Galway on several occasions, including at the Sliding Rock in Shantalla, then some distance outside the city. There were up to 300,000 people in attendance. O'Connell also spoke in Clifden on 17 September 1843. The organisers had constructed a huge pavilion on a high point outside the town and thousands listened enraptured to O'Connell, who spoke both English and Irish, the latter the language of the overwhelming majority of the people at the time. O'Connell died in 1847, without seeing his dream realised.

GALWAY'S POPULATION SKYROCKETS

By 1845, up to 80 per cent of Irish people lived in rural areas and Galway was no different. The county was divided into eighteen baronies – Aran, Athenry, Ballymoe, Ballynahinch, Clare, Clonmacowen, Dunkellin, Dunmore, Galway, Kilconnell, Killian, Kiltartan, Leitrim, Longford, Loughrea, Moycullen, Ross and Tiaquin. All, with the exception of Galway, were overwhelmingly rural and each would see large population increases in the two decades before 1845, by which time there was a population of 442,000 people in the county, the second largest of any county after Cork and well ahead of Dublin at the time. Just one in twenty-five of them lived in what the British government considered to be first-class accommodation and these were usually landlords and their families. By contrast, more than half lived in the lowest class of house; fourth-class dwellings. These people lived in overcrowded conditions on farms of less than 20 acres. Grandparents and members of the extended family also commonly shared the house. The dwellings themselves were often little better than mud huts and could not provide sufficient protection against the unpredictable weather of the west, and the occupants were often in poor health.

The 'Night of the Big Wind' that occurred on 5 January 1839 destroyed hundreds of these homes throughout Galway. The previous evening, a heavy snow had been followed by a howling wind and driving rain. This quickly developed into hurricane-force gales that battered Galway and counties all along the west coast. Throughout the night, most people cowered in their homes and prayed for it to end. The damage was severe. Thousands of chimneys collapsed, multiple roofs were torn off houses, countless trees came crashing onto buildings and hundreds of fires started across the country, often as a result of embers from hearths being blown onto thatched roofs. Newspapers quickly began to report on the carnage, but word from Galway was scant in the days after the storm. There were few newspapers in the west at the time and thus communication was minimal, particularly after a devastating storm such as the one just experienced. A week after the event, the *Dublin Evening Post* stated that there had been 'no news from the exposed coast of Galway', although the *Tuam Herald* said that Oughterard and its environs were a 'scene of misery and woe'. Close to 50,000 trees of ash, oak and elm fell on Mr Kirwan's property near Moylough, while Garbally Park near Ballinasloe was similarly cleared of nearly all trees. There were several deaths in Galway, including of Catherine Reid and Mrs Callanan on Mainguard Street in the city, who were killed when their house collapsed on top of them. Twenty-three fishermen sailing to Carraroe were also lost when caught in the freak storm.

Despite the terrible condition of their homes, farmers paid high rent to their landlords, often most of the pittance they were able to earn at fairs or markets for their produce. Poorer again were labourers who owned no land of their own and worked for farmers, often in return for a tiny plot of land to till. The only saving grace remained the potato, eaten for breakfast, lunch and dinner by the poor. It was the main factor in the population of Galway rising. The small plots of lands ensured that farmers had little room for tillage gardens, relying on the potato and rarely attempting to plant diverse crops. In the 1830s, Samuel Lewis declared himself unimpressed with farming methods in Galway, which he said were in a 'backward' state, although he did praise the areas around Ballinasloe, Tuam and Gort where crop rotation had been introduced. Dutton, who studied Galway in detail, stated that the potato in poor areas was 'the greatest curse she could ever receive', due to its propensity to fail in years of poor weather or disease. In 1845, he was proven to be correct.

5

THE GREAT FAMINE IN COUNTY GALWAY

First Signs of Famine

A severe famine had struck the country in 1822 and there were many deaths throughout Galway. Newspapers reported that 'whole clans were pouring in [to Galway City] from the mountains of Connemara in search of food'. Another source claimed that the people had to resort to 'eating the bark off the trees, the young wheat in the ear and the primrose leaves', while references were made to the swollen limbs and naked bodies of the people. The *Freeman's Journal* reported that families in the county had in desperation killed off and eaten their pigs, geese and hens and afterwards faced imminent starvation. This famine also caused various diseases to spread, but fortunately the following year's harvest was much improved and things slowly got back to normal. The Great Famine that struck in 1845 was unlike anything ever seen, however.

The first sign that something was amiss came when blotches appeared on the leaves and stems of potatoes. These were a result of a fungus called blight that caused half of the crop of 1845 to rot. The overcrowded nature of rural Galway and the poor soil characteristic of the land on the west coast saw the county being one of the worst affected in that year. There was great hardship, but as it was the first time famine had occurred for several years, many people were able to cope. Some had food left over from the previous year's harvest while others were able to fish the lakes and rivers for food. Others picked berries and ate seaweed or sold or pawned their nets, boats and furniture to buy food. The British government, which ruled Ireland at the time, also imported a food known as Indian Meal, which was given out to many poorer people at a low price. This meal was hard to digest and very unpleasant to eat but did have some impact in preventing deaths. The people who had just about survived 1845 looked forward to a better harvest the following year. Tragically, 1846 proved to be devastating.

Very few potatoes could be salvaged from the ground and there was nowhere near enough food to keep tenant families nourished. Most people had used up their food supply and sold many of their worldly possessions the year before. The poorest people, already weakened from 1845, fell ill with terrible diseases and many died due to hunger and disease. Few had money to pay their rent. Some landlords were somewhat sympathetic. Many were not. Marcella Gerrard, a landlord from Ballinlass near Mountbellew, evicted nearly 3,000 of her tenants and ordered sixty homes be demolished. The evicted tenants were reported to be sleeping in ditches. The Gerrards had been advised by neighbouring landlords to give evicted tenants the price of their passage to America. In most cases, they did not do so. Desperation often led to violence, and in the same village in September 1847 Patrick Costello, a 'driver for rent', was murdered and his head 'literally smashed ... to atoms' for bringing proceedings against people for trespass. A new British government in 1846, led by John Russell, also proved disastrous, the new regime taking a hands-off approach, believing that the free market would solve all ills, despite growing reports from Ireland that people were dying in their droves.

The exportation of Irish-grown food also occurred from Galway, despite the desperate conditions locally. As 1846 wore on, many of Galway's poor and starving masses, most notably fishermen from the Claddagh, began to attempt to obstruct the exportation of food. Despite numerous food riots, and the death of at least one woman during them, the exports continued unabated, as did deaths from starvation and disease. The following year, Black '47, is remembered as the worst year of all. Many farmers had been too hungry and poor to plant a crop in 1846 and again very few potatoes were harvested. There was no work other than back-breaking relief work building roads, piers and other infrastructure. This was poorly paid and many of the weakened people were not capable of carrying it out. The toll such arduous toil took is illustrated by the story of one man, Thomas Malone, who dropped dead on the road of hunger and fatigue in 1846. The emaciated Malone had been on the way home after working all day on the road from Casla to Oughterard carrying sandbags for sixpence a day. Cruel landlords continued to evict tenants, leaving bands of starving people wandering the roads. Thousands died at the roadside and famine fever was rampant. In 1847, Tuam was hit by a cholera epidemic that was said to have left corpses on every street.

Workhouses were wretched places where the poorest people who no longer had the means for survival were admitted. The conditions were kept deliberately deplorable to make them unattractive and diseases spread quickly in the overcrowded, slum-like conditions. In Galway, there were workhouses in the city and at Clifden, Oughterard, Loughrea, Gort, Ballinasloe, Portumna, Tuam and Mountbellew, with several smaller auxiliary workhouses being built elsewhere later. All were soon packed to over-flowing. Ballinasloe workhouse was built to accommodate 400 people but was home to more than ten times this number in June 1849. Diseases like cholera were rampant in conditions such as these. The population of County Galway began to plummet as deaths mounted and tens of thousands who could afford to take the emigration boat did so. Some rural dwellers went to live in towns, desperately seeking employment and food. A British Army captain named Hellard reported that in December 1847 'no less than eleven boats, loaded with destitute persons' had arrived at Galway Harbour from Connemara. The census of 1851, taken just as the famine ended, indicated a population of nearly 24,000 people for Galway City, an increase of some 37 per cent since the previous census ten years before. However, 3,732 of those recorded were inmates of public institutions such as the infirmary or the workhouse.

Stories of piles of rotting bodies lying by the roadside or in dilapidated cabins were common as the Famine wore on and Galway became the home of an increasingly desperate populace, some of whom resorted to all sorts of crimes to attempt to stay alive. Murder, theft and violence were frequent. In August 1847, for example, a pig jobber named Lowry was travelling to the Tully Pig Fair. Seeking lodgings on the night before the fair, he stayed with a man named Monahan in the townland of Tooreena. Monahan murdered Lowry as he slept by slitting his throat and then stole his money. When Lowry's family reported him missing, a search of Monahan's house found the body of the unfortunate man concealed underneath the sod wall roof of the house. Monahan died in Galway Gaol before he could be tried. The following year, the body of a 20-year-old Michael Halloran was discovered by his brother in their house near Tuam. Halloran's brother had returned from England and enquired of Michael's whereabouts. It transpired that he had been murdered three months previously by his sister Mary Halloran and his cousin John. Michael's body had then been covered in clay and left rotting in a back room of the house for three months while the killers ate, slept and drank near the corpse.

QUAKERS AND THE BRITISH GOVERNMENT RESPONSE

Quakers were one of the few groups that fully understood the scale of the disaster and they worked hard to save lives in Galway. William E. Forster travelled through the county during the Famine, later recounting the terrible suffering. Forster's petitions for help spurred many Quakers into action. One of them, James Hack Tuke, visited Connemara in 1847 and was appalled by what he saw. Every direction he looked, 'Whole villages were being swept away by emigration.' James and Mary Ellis, two wealthy Quakers from England, left a thriving textile business in their home country to move to the far western village of Letterfrack, where they rented nearly 2,000 acres. They immediately set to work, hiring local people to build a non-denominational school, dispensary, shop and temperance hall. The couple paid reasonable wages and were popular in the locality. In total, they spent eight years in Letterfrack before ill health forced their departure. Letterfrack was in an area of Connemara that lost almost half its population during the Famine, yet its own population remained steady in the worst years of the catastrophe due to the Ellises. Colmanstown in east Galway was similarly transformed by Quakers, who spent £12,000 converting a patch of land outside the village into a model farm that employed hundreds of local people and taught them modern farming techniques.

Government funding for soup kitchens throughout the county, which were feeding 3 million a day nationally, was withdrawn unexpectedly in August 1847, the powers that be announcing that they expected the coming harvest to be much improved, something that did not come to pass. Nevertheless, the Quakers continued to feed as many of the starving masses as they could. Asenath Nicolson was another visitor to Galway in these years. A philanthropist from a wealthy American Protestant family, Nicholson was horrified by the poverty she witnessed in Galway, describing the county as a 'place of filth, poverty and disease'. She nevertheless lodged with the people who, despite being on the verge of starvation, were helpful and generous. In one cottage near the village of Claddaghduff, she described how after she entered:

> Every spade was dropped, and in a few moments the ground of the cabin was packed with men, women, and children, in rags and tatters. They sat down upon their haunches, and began their welcomes to Ireland, and their wonder that so 'goodly a body should leave so fine a country to see such a poor people. And sure ye must be hungry – and such a dacent body wouldn't ait a potato?' Assuring them I was not hungry, they all rose and joined in one universal valedictory of, 'God bless ye, and speed ye on yer journey.'[9]

Like the Quakers, Nicholson gave as much help as she could. The Choctaw and Cherokee nations, despite having just been removed from their ancestral lands in America, sent a remarkable $800. The Sultan of the Ottoman Empire sent £1,000 and five shiploads of food. This help, while welcome, was nowhere near enough to avert the catastrophe and the British government's response was sadly deficient.

9   Nicolson, A. (1847), *Ireland's Welcome to the Stranger*, p.411.

Doctors were in short supply and faced great danger from famine fever. At least eleven doctors died in Galway in 1847, including Charles Donnellan of Annaghdown and Edward Lambert of Oranmore.

Those who could afford to emigrate were generally the lucky ones, although many would die on the overcrowded and unsanitary coffin ships. One hundred famine ships sailed from Galway Port alone between the years 1847 and 1850, bound for America, England and beyond. These famine emigrants from the county travelled all over the world and large groups of Galway people could be found congregated in all the large cities of the English-speaking world. From 1849 onwards, the potato crop slowly returned to normal, although some effects of the Famine lasted until 1851. During the disaster, 1 million Irish people died of starvation and disease, while close to 2 million may have emigrated. Galway lost a third of its population during this unmitigated human catastrophe. Every area suffered – just one example was Loughrea, which between the years 1841 and 1861 went from a population of 5,458 down to 3,074.

The Emigrants' Farewell (from *An Illustrated History of Ireland* by Mary Frances Cusack).

Many emigrants who left Galway travelled to other lands, where they had an impact on their new home. Many Galway men fought on either side in the Mexican–American War of 1846–48, for example. John O'Reilly of Ballyconneely, Co. Galway, famously helped to form the San Patricios Brigade of the Mexican Army. Not all immigrants from Galway chose to enlist. Patrick Sarsfield Gilmore, born in Ballygar, Co. Galway, in 1829, emigrated to America in 1847. Having learned the cornet at a young age, the Galway native quickly got work in a music shop in Boston before joining the city's brass band. His talent was unmistakable and Gilmore enlisted in the Northern Army in the American Civil War, during which he published the words and music for 'When Johnny Comes Marching Home', a song that soon grew to national prominence. Gilmore became famous throughout America and in 1869 organised an enormous peace jubilee aimed at uniting the country after the war. It had an orchestra of 1,000 musicians, conducted by Gilmore himself, and hundreds of thousands of spectators were present. Gilmore died suddenly while touring in 1892 but is still remembered, in Galway and in America, as a pioneering musician who escaped the Famine and changed the course of musical history.

Ireland in Post-Famine Times

The Famine did not prove the end of Ireland's trials and tribulations. Many landlords had gone bankrupt during the disaster and were forced to sell up their estates. The Martin estate in Connemara, formerly comprising 200,000 acres and the largest property in Ireland or Britain, was broken up and sold on, for example. It was often difficult to find buyers for these estates and most of those who did eventually invest were not members of the traditional gentry – they were insurance companies or financial interests who were wholly unsentimental to their tenants and in many ways worse than those that they replaced. Nearly all Galway landlords experienced financial difficulty, although many held on to their estates. Among those who remained in situ, some were despised for the way they had dealt with their starving tenantry during the Famine. A small number could be described as 'improving landlords'. These charged fair rent and invested in their properties to improve the lives of the tenantry. Even if a tenant was fortunate enough to have such a landlord, poor prospects, large families and occasional crop failure meant that few could prosper. Emigration continued to ravage Galway's countryside in the 1850s and beyond. Numbers living in Galway City did grow, although the conditions of housing were scarcely better than that in the countryside and life in urban areas was disease ridden and dangerous and jobs remained in short supply.

One route out of this poverty-stricken life was to join the British Army, which was always recruiting. There was a Regiment of Foot raised in Galway in the 1790s, replaced by the Connacht Rangers, which catered specifically for those from Galway and the west of Ireland. It was one of eight regiments raised largely in Ireland, and had its headquarters at Renmore in Galway City. Britain, which had an ever-expanding empire in the nineteenth century, was perpetually at war or putting down uprisings and had an insatiable desire for recruits. Galway proved a fertile hunting ground. The Crimean War, which occurred in the decade after the Famine, was one example of a conflict featuring many Galway soldiers. Two cannon reputedly taken from the Russians during the Battle of Inkerman in 1854 were presented to Galway City for its support during the war and subsequently took pride of place in Eyre Square, where they remain to this day.

The workers of Galway City also benefitted from several institutions that were placed there in light of it being the most significant urban area in the west. Queen's College, Galway, was completed in 1849. It was one of three Queen's Colleges nationally, along with Belfast and Cork. Initially, it had an intake of just sixty-eight pupils and only arts, medicine and law were offered as subjects. It was rejected by the Catholic Church as 'Godless' and it took several decades before the Church gave the new institution its blessing. This was welcomed by many Catholics who were keen to gain an education, seen by many as their only option of progressing. A new system of national education had been established in 1831 and, by the 1850s, the levels of literacy in Galway were growing, a trend that continued throughout the century. Correspondingly, the number of people speaking English was also growing at the expense of Irish, which in many people's minds was associated with poverty. Galway, nevertheless, remained the county with the highest percentage of Irish speakers.

The location of Galway County Courthouse, built in 1815, also provided employment for the denizens of the city, as did the erection of another bridge over the Corrib connecting the courthouse to the gaol on the other side of the river. These courts were busy, there being more than 200 offences punishable by death as late as 1830. Public hangings were held in Galway at this time and were a major social event. John Hurley, for example, was hanged for the murder of Catherine Kendrigan in 1853 in front of an esti-mated 2,000 people at Galway Gaol. The law was charged in 1868 and hangings went behind closed doors. The last hanging was that of Thomas Keeley in 1903 for the murder of Mary Clasby in Athenry. The Galway County Infirmary was another institution that employed nurses and doctors, and had other benefits for the local economy. It was built at Prospect Hill in the city and opened in 1802. Not all institutions were placed in Galway City, however. The notorious Lunatic Asylum for the Province of Connacht was erected in Ballinasloe in 1843 at a cost of £27,000.

ECONOMIC OPPORTUNITIES FOR GALWAY

Another potential economic opportunity for Galway lay in establishing the city as one of the main European transatlantic hubs and making it suitable for larger vessels. Hardiman stated in 1820 that 'the haven is safe and spacious and is capable of affording protection to the largest of fleets'. Galway was located some 300 miles closer to the American coast than the English port of Liverpool and there were real opportunities to claim some of the transatlantic market. In the 1830s, major infrastructural works were undertaken to improve the harbour, and large-scale reclamation of land from the sea took place. There were transatlantic services intermittently, especially during the Famine, and between 1880 and 1905 the Allan Line operated a mail and passenger service with America.

There was potential for other water-based travel in the county and the Eglinton Canal was built in the 1840s. This provided another connection between Lough Corrib and the sea. Meanwhile, efforts were being made to dig out a canal connecting Lough Mask to Lough Corrib. This would allow boats to travel all the way from near Castlebar in Co. Mayo to Galway Bay, a 40-mile journey that would have been of great benefit to those living on the shores of the lake in towns such as Headford and Oughterard. It was discovered mid-construction that there were several problems with the project – foremost among them was the porous limestone soil between the two lakes that caused the water to drain away. The lakes were also at different heights, meaning the builders were attempting to make the water flow uphill. Finally, railways were being built all over the country, undermining the importance of travel and commerce on the water. The project was eventually abandoned and the Dublin–Galway railway line was opened in 1851. It ran through Ballinasloe, Athenry and Oranmore, helping these towns to grow and making the city more accessible. It mitigated the difficulties in Galway's remote location, making the county more attractive to both tourists and industry. It also carried emigrants from Galway to Dublin and other ports, however, aiding them in leaving their home forever.

Not all emigrants from Galway were escaping poverty. Some sought adventure in the uncharted parts of the world. Robert O'Hara Burke was one example. Born into a land-owning family at Issercleran House, near Loughrea, Co. Galway, in 1821, Robert was an adventurous young man and enlisted in the British Army during the Crimean War before deciding to emigrate to Australia. He became a well-regarded police-man in his adopted country and when the government of Victoria sponsored an expedition across the Australian continent from south to north

Robert O'Hara Burke (from *Australian Heroes and Adventurers* by William Pyke).

in 1860, many Australians believed that endless gold was waiting to be found. Burke applied to lead the expedition, hoping to become the first European to chart such a course. He had little experience of the Australian Bush. Nevertheless, he and his initially large group of men were successful and reached the northern coast in February 1861 after a gruelling 1,500-mile journey. By this stage, the party featured only Burke and three others. They became disorientated and run out of food on the journey home, Burke dying on 30 June 1861. His body was discovered after a thorough search and the Galway man was honoured with an Australian state funeral.

RELIGION IN COUNTY GALWAY

The Catholic Church was also growing in importance throughout Galway in the years after the Famine. It became better organised and trained more priests. Increasingly, having a son in the priesthood was considered a great honour. Several Galway clergymen went on to make their mark nationally and internationally, including Fr Tom Burke, known as 'Prince of the Preachers' for the fame his oratory earned him in America, and Fr Edward Flanagan of Ballymoe, Co. Galway, who emigrated to the same country in 1904 and founded 'Boys' Town' in Omaha, Nebraska, in 1922, a community that fed, clothed and educated thousands of boys from underprivileged backgrounds and which became known for the slogan 'There is no such thing as a bad boy.'

Galway was overwhelmingly Catholic but there remained a small number of Protestants. Although sectarianism was not something associated with the county, it did occur on occasion, especially when proselytisers were operating there. These proselytisers were Protestant missionaries who attempted to tempt poverty-stricken Catholics into converting to Protestantism in exchange for food and clothing. They also provided free education in mission schools to children in exchange for Protestant scripture reading. Such schools were established all over Co. Galway. In the years following the Famine, for example, a total of sixty-four mission stations were established in west Connemara. These proved fruitful at times of poor harvests, such as 1863 when it was reported that the people were burning furze for warmth in the winter after a wet summer. Anyone who converted to Protestantism was called a 'souper' and attracted much hostility. Clashes between priests and missionaries occurred, most famously on Omey Island in 1879 when William MacNeice, a teacher at a mission school, pushed the parish priest out of his schoolhouse. MacNeice stated that the curate had entered, shouting that he had come 'in search of any stray sheep'. An angry crowd, on hearing that the priest had been assaulted, attacked the teacher. This unleashed a wave of attacks on mission schools and churches and a hundred extra police were quickly drafted in to restore the peace. This was a relatively unusual occurrence, however, and relationships between the two communities was usually civil, if distant.

6

THE LAND WAR AND A GAELIC REVIVAL IN THE WEST

THE FENIAN REBELLION AND GALWAY POLITICS

There remained huge discontent with the land situation in the late 1860s but ordinary people could do little to change the status quo, as most had little say in choosing their political leaders. By then, only the wealthiest one sixth of Irishmen (and no Irishwomen) were entitled to vote. This dissatisfaction would lead to another short-lived rebellion in 1867, masterminded by a group known as the Fenians, a movement that sought independence by whatever means necessary. The 1867 Rising ultimately petered out with little success after a few minor skirmishes. Galway saw little action, although Thomas J. Kelly of Mountbellew was one of the Rising's main architects. Kelly served with the Union Army in the American Civil War before returning to Ireland. His wartime experience shaped him and he began to resent the injustices faced by Irish people. He soon became one of the main figures in the Fenians and travelled to England, planning to storm Chester Castle, take away any available weapons and start a guerilla war in England. The plan was eventually aborted but Kelly was arrested in September. As he was being transported in a prison van, three Fenians stormed the vehicle, shooting a policeman and freeing Kelly. The Galwayman managed to escape but his three rescuers were arrested, tried, found guilty and hanged, later becoming known as the Manchester Martyrs. Kelly was smuggled out of the country and lived out his life in America. In the wake of the 1867 Rising, the police in Galway feared that there remained potential for conflict. The cannon in Eyre Square were temporarily removed to the barracks in Athlone for fear the Fenians would repurpose them and use them in the rebellion, a fear that proved unfounded.

By the early 1870s, violence as a method of achieving independence had been largely forgotten and Home Rule was the new objective for most Irish people. The aim of the Home Rule movement was simple – a parliament in Dublin, something that the British parliament in Westminster seemed unlikely to grant. Meanwhile, local politics was occupying the minds of Galway natives, despite the fact that most could not cast a vote. The Galway election of 1872 was particularly important. Before that point, the few tenants who could vote supported the political candidate favoured by their landlord, but in 1872, John Philip Nolan ran on a campaign in the Galway election that promised to restrict the power of landlords and curtail their ability to carry out unlimited evictions. This was hugely popular among ordinary Galwegians. His conservative opponent, Captain La Poer Trench, preferred the status quo and was the chosen candidate of most landlords throughout the county. In his memoirs, a Galway priest named Fr Eugene Nevin described La Poer Trench as 'a bigoted Protestant who stood for extermination, landlordism and shameless proselytism'. Nolan won in a landslide. Although he was ultimately unseated by the courts due to the priests' alleged 'undue influence' on his campaign, major cracks in the largely deferential relations between landlord and tenant had started to show and the tenants' power and demands grew. Two poor harvests in 1877 and 1878 raised fears that Galway could suffer another famine like the one that had occurred in the 1840s. A new movement was inaugurated in 1879 and Galway was about to enter its most violent phase in modern times.

The Land War Begins in Galway

In 1879, the Land War began in Mayo when a group called the Land League was founded. The League demanded tenant ownership, many believing it was the first step to greater independence. What started as a small group of tenants refusing to pay their rent under the command of a man named Michael Davitt spread throughout the country. Galway, which suffered under similar conditions to neighbouring Mayo, had a long history of standing up for its rights and was one of the first counties in which the movement exploded. Galway natives such as Thomas Ashe were quick to spread the Land League throughout the county. The League demanded the three Fs for tenants: fair rent, free sale and fixity of tenure. Davitt and the Land League threw in their lot with Wicklow politician Charles Stewart Parnell, the main agitator for Home Rule at the time, and boycotting and withholding of rent were chosen as effective tactics to achieve their aims. Mitchell Henry, owner of the salubrious Kylemore Castle, for example, saw his tenants coming together in 1880 and refusing to pay him rent, while intimidating other tenants who were thought to be paying. Landlords, in many cases, refused to give in to these demands and lower the rents demanded. In some cases, they ordered mass evictions against non-paying tenants instead. Multiple tenants of villages such as Carraroe and

Ballyconneely in Connemara and Woodford in east Galway were served with eviction notices. Mass protests against these evictions were organised. In Carraroe, in January 1880, a force of up to seventy police was dispatched to the village tasked with serving eviction notices on 150 houses on the impoverished Kirwan Estate, which was described by the village's own land agent as the 'most inaccessible and least advantageously situated spot in the whole of Ireland'.

Ultimately, more than a thousand people gathered in Carraroe to stop the evictions happening. Many were from the immediate area, but people had also travelled from other communities, by boat and on foot, to support their fellow tenants. After just four notices of evictions were served, the crowd began to shout denunciations of the police, the process server and the landlord. A furious police sergeant produced a sword and held it aloft, shouting at the crowd – it was taken from him swiftly and smashed into pieces. A violent clash then ensued and sticks, stones and other projectiles were hurled at police. Three policemen were injured, along with the bailiff. As one letter writer to the *Tuam Herald* said at the time, 'A Connemara woman with a sock full of stones is a match for four policemen.'

These tactics were repeated in villages throughout the county, forcing landlords to concede to local demands. Boycotting landlords who refused to drop the rent was also a common tactic and many Galway landlords found themselves unable to get service in local shops or to find local people to work in their fields. Threatening letters were sent, barns were burned and animals were harmed. In more serious instances, violence was used in Galway. Landlords and anyone who worked for them, especially land agents, were in danger. J.H. Tuke, a Quaker and philanthropist, arriving in Galway during the Land War, stated that land agents 'ducked instinctively or lashed their horse when passing any thick bushes to avoid bullets which may arrive at any minute'.[10]

He added that in the west of Ireland, he found a lawless land where murderers roamed free, tolerated by the priests, everyone else too afraid to denounce them. Although violence was condemned by the Land League, it occurred regularly and Galway was considered the third most disturbed county, in a country riven by strife, between 1880 and 1882.

FATALITIES AND FURTHER VIOLENCE

A major early fatality of the Land War was the shooting in September 1880 of Lord Mountmorres, the landlord of a small estate near Clonbur, 30 miles west of Galway City. The Letterfrack Murders of April 1881 also catapulted the county to international attention. In this incident, two herders for the local landlord, John and Matin Lydon, were taken from their beds and shot dead. In February 1882, Constable James Kavanagh, who had been investigating the murder, was also shot dead as he left a public house. Patrick Walsh, a neighbour of the Lydons, was found guilty of the killing and hanged in Galway Gaol in September 1882. Several others would receive ten years in jail for conspiracy. Walsh's brother Michael was later sentenced to death for the Kavanagh shooting, although he was probably just 15 years of age and his sentence was eventually commuted to penal servitude for life. Both men protested their innocence to the last and evidence against them was scant.

More murders and outrages followed, including the Huddy Murders at Cloughbrack in Connemara, when a

10 Kavanagh, J. (2021), *The Irish Assassins*, p.85.

land agent, Joseph Huddy, and his 17-year-old grandson John, were shot dead and thrown into Lough Mask on 3 January 1882 when they were handing out ejectment notices. The Huddys were unpopular and police believed that the entire village of Cloughbrack had revolted against the process servers, shooting them dead and concealing their bodies in the lake. Nobody would admit to having even seen the men, however, and it was four days before the bodies were recovered from the watery depths. Eventually one villager spoke out and implicated three other local men in the killing. All men were Irish speakers and had difficulty following the court proceedings. They were found guilty nonetheless. Patrick Higgins was hanged on 16 January 1883, just over a year after the Lough Mask Murders. Thomas Higgins and Michael Flynn were hanged the following day, all protesting their innocence.

The most famous Irish outrage of the nineteenth century, the Phoenix Park Murders of May 1882, also had a strong Galway connection, despite occurring in the capital. Frederick Cavendish, Chief Secretary for Ireland and thus the country's most important politician, was stabbed to death in Phoenix Park along with his undersecretary, Thomas Henry Burke, a native of Tuam and the initial target of the attack. Burke was the most important civil servant in Ireland and nicknamed 'the Castle Rat' for his work in upholding the British system. Five men were hanged for this crime.

Another terrible Galway affair occurred on 17 August 1882, just a few miles from Cloughbrack, in the lonely valley of Maamtrasna. The home of John Joyce, his wife Bridget, his mother Margaret, his daughter Peggy and his son Michael was broken into and the occupants beaten and shot dead. Another son, Patsy, miraculously survived the attack. The motive was unclear but likely agrarian in nature and the police clamoured to apprehend the culprits. Within days, three local men came forward to say that they had been awoken on the night of the slaughter by a party of ten men passing their house and that they had followed them to the Joyce household, standing outside as the massacre unfolded. This story was highly dubious but eight men were convicted of the infamous murder and three would ultimately hang: Patrick Joyce, Pat Casey and Maolra Seoige (Myles Joyce), the latter of whom was completely innocent and exonerated by the Irish state some 135 years after his death. There were growing protests in Connemara that the British justice system was punishing people with Land League backgrounds for agrarian crimes committed, even if the evidence against them was not convincing.

OUTRAGES IN EAST GALWAY

East Galway was equally dangerous, particularly the area in a triangle from Ardrahan to Craughwell to Loughrea, although securing convictions there was proving even more difficult than in Connemara. It began with intimidation, such as when the landlord John Lambert of Aggard House near Craughwell woke up to find a grave had been dug in the garden in front of his house. The local hunt, a favourite pastime of the gentry, was also disrupted regularly in protest at many landlords' refusals to lower the cost of rent. Like Connemara, however, more violent methods were also utilised and there was a spate of violent deaths in the space of a little over a year between mid-1881 and the summer of 1882. James Connors was the first to be shot in May 1881, having taken a job working for Lord Dunsandle despite having been warned not to do so. Peter Dempsey was then shot on the way to Mass two weeks later for occupying a boycotted farm at Riverville near Craughwell. In July, a policeman named Constable Linton was gunned down at Loughrea, while the following June a landlord named Walter Bourke of Rahasane was ambushed and shot dead. Bourke was unpopular and had conducted numerous evictions during the Land War. There is evidence that he feared for his life and he had taken the precaution of having a bodyguard, Robert Wallace, with him at all times, but he too was shot and killed.

Later that month, John Henry Blake, an agent of Lord Clanricarde, was shot dead in broad daylight near Loughrea. Absentee landlord Clanricarde was one of the biggest land-owners in the country, possessing an enormous holding of more than 50,000 acres, stretching from Meelick in the east of the county to Derrybrien in the south. He rarely visited his vast estate and was widely despised, having a reputation as an evicting landlord. Opportunities to attack Clanricarde were not forthcoming, so a party of men planned an attack on Blake, a native of Furbo and a regular visitor to the local tenantry demanding rent. Blake, his wife Henrietta, and their servant, Thady Ruane, were on their way to church in Loughrea in June 1882 when armed men emerged from the fields and shot both Blakes and Ruane. The two men died. Henrietta was wounded but survived.

Although the Land League continued to publicly denounce violence, the authorities blamed them for the outrages and several baronies in Co. Galway found themselves proclaimed and placed under a form of martial law. Several figures in the Land League were arrested and charges brought in several cases. The only punishments meted out were for the shooting of a man named Peter Doherty near Craughwell in November 1881, however. Doherty had been in dispute over a small holding locally and was being boycotted. He was shot in his front yard after hearing a noise outside and going out to investigate. Two local men, Michael Muldowney and Patrick Finnegan, were convicted and sentenced to death in 1884. Both protested their innocence and eventually had their sentences commuted.

CONSEQUENCES OF THE LAND WAR

The Land War was over by 1882 and Galway slowly returned to an uneasy peace. There had been some concessions made to tenants in the form of Land Acts that slightly improved the lot of some, but simultaneously harsh new legislation was introduced in the form of two Coercion Acts. These acts permitted the arrest of anyone suspected of agitating for land reform. Hundreds of arrests were made in Galway, particularly in the Loughrea area, on foot of these new laws. The turmoil of the 1879–81 period saw some landlords change their ways, although others refused to budge. Lord Clanricarde hired a new agent, Frank Joyce, after Blake's shooting. Joyce was provided with four constables and was told to collect all rent due without accepting any excuse. This proved highly unpopular and matters came to a head in 1886 in the Woodford area when four tenants, who owed a combined total of £128, were to be evicted. Although the Land League refused to get involved, the local people and the parish priest supported the men. No locals would aid in carrying out the evictions and Joyce was forced to summon 500 police from Dublin. They found the roads blocked with trees and boulders and struggled to even reach Woodford. When they finally got to their destination, they were met by thousands of local tenants, who refused to allow the eviction to occur. Hives of bees, boiling water and boulders were used to hinder the eviction process. After a sustained battle, policemen eventually gained entry through the roof. Several protesters were arrested. One of them, Tommy Larkin, died in prison and it was said that 20,000 attended his funeral.

The Land War scarcely improved the situation in poverty-stricken Connemara. When, in 1882, J.H. Tuke offered an assisted emigration scheme from the region to the New World, he was inundated with applications. Whole families were encouraged and those considered suitable had their passage paid to Canada, Minnesota and other northern American areas. Hundreds made this trip, never to return. This policy was considered by Tuke as good for both those who left and those who stayed in Connemara, the latter possibly being able to avail of the now vacant land. Not everyone was pleased with this orchestrated emigration policy, however – the *Freeman's Journal* newspaper stated that 'Connemara is meant for man, not just beasts.'

THE CONGESTED DISTRICTS BOARD

One worthwhile effort of the government to improve the lot of the people was the foundation of the Congested Districts Board in 1891. These specially chosen districts were largely rural areas on the west coast with high populations and poor land. The board's role was to improve such areas by providing industry and building houses. Eventually, almost the entirety of County Galway was under the jurisdiction of the board. A Major Ruttledge-Fair, on visiting the parish of Ballinakill, observed that:

> The families remain largely self-supporting. They grow their own vegetables and most have some livestock; perhaps two cows and two pigs, and some geese or chicken. Eggs are valuable and generally sold by the families to egg dealers. People rise early here and

are often in bed again by 9pm. Houses are generally in a poor condition and have no chimneys. Most supplies, including flour, meal and drapery, are got from the shops here on credit between Christmas and July. This credit is charged at interest rates between 10 and 20 per cent. A bad season often meant that families could only pay a portion of their debt. Two bad seasons in a row generally spelled trouble for both customer and shopkeeper as the latter's resources are stretched also. Money remains scarce.[11]

The board also provided teachers to come into coastal areas and teach net mending and boat building. Elsewhere, they established schools, provided thread for lacemakers and gave looms and spinning wheels on credit. Any clothes produced were then sold on, providing extra income for the families. The CDB, which remained in existence until 1923, also saw the construction of hundreds of better-quality houses throughout Galway.

11 Congested Districts Board Outline Report (1891) – Ballinakill.

A newly built Congested Districts Board house, *c.*1908 (from *One Irish Summer* by William Curtis).

A Gaelic Revival in the West

Despite definite improvements in the quality of life of the people, there remained political tensions at the end of the nineteenth century. Ireland being ruled from London was still unpopular and the majority of Galway people remained hopeful that Home Rule and a parliament in Dublin would be granted. Ireland had a unique identity and culture, and most people felt the island should have some form of self-determination. It was becoming increasingly clear that many traditional Irish pastimes were dying out, however. This realisation spearheaded a reawakening of interest in Irish culture, something that brought about fundamental changes to how the Irish saw themselves. Galway, as arguably the Gaelic capital of Ireland and a guardian of traditions thousands of years old, was at the forefront of this change.

The Gaelic Athletic Association (The GAA)

One of the first aspects of Irish culture to be revitalised was sport. Sport in Galway had changed much over the eighteenth and nineteenth centuries and English sports such as cricket, sponsored by landlords, had become popular by the mid-nineteenth century, pushing older pastimes such as hurling into ever-smaller pockets of the south-east of the county. The founding of the Gaelic Athletic Association in Co. Tipperary in 1884 changed everything. The GAA aimed to reinstate traditionally Irish pastimes such as Gaelic football and hurling as the main sports played. One of the most important figures in the GAA was Michael Cusack, a Clareman who had been principal teacher of Lough Cutra National School near Gort in Co. Galway for several years, where he taken a huge interest in local Gaelic sports and pastimes. The GAA was astonishingly successful and the ancient game of hurling retook precedence within a few years of its establishment, eventually overtaking cricket in popularity in the south and east of Galway.

One of the first matches played under the Gaelic Athletic Association banner was a hurling match said to have taken place in Beagh in the extreme south of the county. Galway were also represented in the first all-Ireland hurling final in 1887 by the Meelick-Eyrecourt club. They lost to Tipperary outfit Thurles Sarsfields on a scoreline of 1-1 to 0-0. Ardrahan and Peterswell were also very successful in the early years, winning many of the first two dozen titles after the competition's inauguration in 1887. However, Castlegar, on the eastern outskirts of the city, are now the most successful team, having won seventeen county titles. Eventually, it was decided that the best players from each club should come together to form county teams and Galway was blessed with talent. They tasted all-Ireland success for the first time in 1923.

Another ancient sport, Gaelic football, was played in the county long before the foundation of the GAA but the organisation helped to codify and streamline the rules. They also organised competitions. Unlike hurling, football's heartland was in the north of the county and in Connemara. The first club championship was played in 1889 and Tuam Stars, Dunmore McHales and St Grellans, Ballinasloe were the most successful teams in the early years. Galway won their first all-Ireland football title two years after the hurlers in 1925.

THE GAELIC LEAGUE (*CONRADH NA GAEILGE*)

The Irish language was another aspect of Gaelic culture that appeared to be in terminal decline in Galway. In 1800, there were more Irish speakers globally than those of Swedish, Finnish or Dutch. Throughout Galway at that time, practically everyone was an Irish speaker, many having no command of English whatsoever. Galway City was something of an exception, with English being strong. Pressure was growing on the language, however. By 1850, portions of the south-east of County Galway had become largely English speaking, and by 1900 most of the area on the east of the Corrib had English as the predominant language. By the 1911 census, the only monoglot Irish speakers left were found in isolated areas west of Lough Corrib.

The reasons behind this rapid decline were manifold. Firstly, the Famine disproportionately affected the poorer, more Irish-speaking west. As well as this, in a county where emigration was a likely outcome for a child once they reached adulthood, English was seen as being of great benefit, Irish as an impediment. There was also a negative attitude to the language among many clergy in the Catholic Church and politicians like Daniel O'Connell, while most schools did not teach Irish at all at this time. All these factors played a huge role in cementing the perception of English as being civilised and modern compared to old-fashioned Irish. The following story, told by folklorist William Wilde, father of Oscar and long-time resident of Galway, displays this attitude clearly.

When arriving to an unnamed Connemara village in the 1840s, Wilde described how:

> A boy of about eight years uttered a short sentence in Irish to his sister. The man called the child to him and drew forth from his dress a little stick and put a small notch in it with a little penknife.

Upon enquiring, we were told that it was done to prevent the children speaking Irish and every time a child attempted it, a nick was placed in the stick. When the child reached a certain number, summary punishment was inflicted by the schoolmaster.

We asked the father if he did not love the Irish language. Indeed, the man scarcely spoke any other. 'I do,' said he, 'sure it is the talk of the old country and the language of my father and the speech of the mountains, lakes and glens where I was bred and born. But you know,' he continued 'the children must have learning and as they teach no Irish in the national school, we must instigate them to talk English.'[12]

In 1893, *Conradh na Gaelige* (The Gaelic League) was set up. Douglas Hyde, the son of a Roscommon rector, was among its founders and he regularly visited Connemara, where the language was at its strongest. Many emigrants had returned to Galway in the late nineteenth century, bringing the English language with them, however, and even west Connemara was struggling to maintain Irish as the community language. In 1908, the newspaper of the Gaelic League, *An Claidheamh Soluis*, stated:

Irish remains spoken on the rugged slopes of the Twelve Bens but beyond, to the west, it has retreated from more open country, leaving behind but scattered traces. The grandparents will generally have the native tongue fluently at their command. The parents will be at home in either language, but speak English, unless to their elders. The children are not unable to follow an Irish speaker, but rarely use an Irish phrase themselves unless they cannot help it.[13]

12 Wilde, W. (1867), *Wilde's Lough Corrib*, p.124.

13 *An Claidheamh Soluis*, 25 April 1908.

Many Galway people were determined to arrest the slide in the language and worked hard for its revival. This included Mícheál Breathnach, a native of Inverin, who wrote and travelled widely, spreading the idea that Irish should be treated with the same love and respect as all modern European languages. Tomás Bán O Conceanainn was another strong Galway advocate of the language. The native of Inis Meáin was the Gaelic League's main organiser in County Galway and at one stage collected $20,000 for the organisation on a tour of America. In 1909, *Coláiste Connacht* was founded in Spiddal, an early example of an Irish language college, where thousands flocked to learn the language.

The League set up hundreds of branches throughout the country, many of the teachers being native speakers from Galway. They also had some success in ensuring the language was introduced as a subject to various schools and colleges throughout the country. After the turn of the century, unthinkably, Irish had started to come back into fashion among many, particularly the Catholic middle class and those who favoured an independent Ireland. This was of undoubted benefit to Galway. By 1911, nearly everyone in the county could speak English and yet more than 54 per cent of the county's population indicated that they could speak Irish also, easily the highest proportion of any county. People interested in the language flocked to Galway to test out their command of the language with the native speakers. This was helpful to the economy, but also began to positively impact how people felt about their native tongue.

THE IRISH LITERARY REVIVAL

A third arm of this revival of Irish culture, and another one strongly associated with County Galway, was the literary revival. By the late nineteenth century, many of the plays and books consumed by Irish people were written by English people and based on English topics. This alarmed a coterie of Irish writers, many of them from Anglo-Irish or wealthy landed backgrounds, who decided to record and reinvigorate Irish stories and attempt to bring them to the masses. The centre of this whole movement was Coole Park near the town of Gort. Coole Park was owned by Lady Gregory, whom George Bernard Shaw once described as the 'greatest living Irishwoman'. Lady Gregory had been born Isabella Augusta Persse into a wealthy family in 1852, growing up at Roxborough House near Loughrea. Her family were interested in local history and Isabella was captivated by the life of the tenants. She married William Gregory in 1880. Gregory owned the leafy estate at Coole Park and his wife took great inspiration from the beautiful surroundings. On her husband's death in 1893, Lady Gregory began to travel around the west collecting old stories and publishing several books of folklore. Lady Gregory also helped to found the Abbey

Theatre, Dublin, along with fellow Galwegian Edward Martyn. The pair encouraged Irish authors and playwrights to write plays based on the Irish experience.

Lady Gregory (from *Irish Plays and Playwrights* by Cornelius Weygandt).

A sketch of Thoor Ballylee by Robert Gregory (from *Visions and Beliefs in the West of Ireland*).

Eventually, Lady Gregory developed many literary connections and her home began to play host to the most famous Irish writers of the day, including W.B. Yeats, John Millington Synge and George Bernard Shaw. These writers also took inspiration from Galway. J.M. Synge moved to the Aran Islands and he wrote many of his most famous works based on the characters he met there, most notably the play *The Playboy of the Western World*. Yeats also resided in Galway, buying a sixteenth-century tower house named Thoor Ballylee, just 4 miles from Coole Park. Some of his most acclaimed works were set in the area, including the poem 'The Wild Swans at Coole'. Lady Gregory died aged 80 in 1932. Sadly, Coole House was demolished shortly afterwards, despite the huge history associated with it. Nevertheless, the Irish Literary Revival had changed the perception of Irish writers and the general public and it ensured that the Irish experience began to take centre stage in the country's literature.

ART AND COUNTY GALWAY

Art was also experiencing a renaissance in Ireland in the late nineteenth and early twentieth century, and Galway was a county much frequented by artists who were attracted there due to its unique landscapes and people. Connemara was to the forefront, the last remnants of the region's ancient culture attracting painters from all over the world. Artists had been coming to Connemara for decades – Frederic William Burton painted there regularly in the pre-Famine years, producing such masterpieces as *A Joyce Country Painting* and *The Aran Fisherman's Drowned Child*, but the 1880s would see an explosion in the number of painters arriving on the west coast. Aloysius O'Kelly took up residence near Leenane for several years and painted many works based on the lives of the local people, including *Mass in a Connemara Cabin*, a painting that received international renown. W.H. Bartlett painted *The Last Brief Voyage, A Connemara Funeral* in 1887, while in the same year Ernest Waterlow's *The Galway Gossips* was widely acclaimed and would hang in the Tate Gallery for decades.

Paul Henry was one of the most influential landscape painters of the twentieth century and many of his most famous paintings were done in Connemara, having spent over a decade living in the west of Ireland. His wife Grace was also a prolific artist who frequently used Connemara as her muse. Other well-known artists who painted Galway were Walter Osborne, Harry Kernoff and Sophie Pemberton. Connemara was not the only part of Galway to feature in artworks – the Claddagh in Galway was painted frequently, perhaps most famously by Paul Henry, while Jack Butler Yeats used the village of Kinvara as a backdrop. Galway also had several well-known home-grown artists – Joseph Haverty among them. Haverty was one of the most successful portrait painters in Ireland in the mid-nineteenth century and his work *The Blind Piper* was critically acclaimed. Tuam painter Augustus Burke's *A Connemara Girl* was another of the most identifiable paintings in Ireland in the early 1870s.

7

EVERYDAY LIFE IN GALWAY AT THE TURN OF THE CENTURY

EMIGRATION, MARRIAGE AND PROGRESS

In the first decade of the twentieth century, County Galway's population continued to decline. Between 1901 and 1911, it dropped a further 5 per cent to 182,000, well under half of what it had been just seventy years before. Even Galway City's population dropped slightly, with economic opportunities limited there by the closing of Persse's Distillery in 1908 and the rapid decline of fishing in the Claddagh area. The population of Ireland had been declining steadily, despite very high birth rates, and it is believed that 4.5 million people emigrated from the country between 1845 and 1922. One out of two people from Connacht are thought to have gone abroad in this time frame. Newspapers of the time carried regular advertisements from Galway shops announcing the stocking of tickets for various shipping lines to America. Other emigrants travelled to the UK, Canada, the USA, Australia and New Zealand. Most did not return.

The conditions for those who stayed in rural Galway were difficult. Men who were promised the farm, usually the oldest son, often stayed at home, living with his parents until his father became too old to work the farm or died. These men consequently married much later, regularly to women considerably younger than themselves. Dowries were usually given to the women due to be married and these were paid on their marriage to the suitable candidate. Large families invariably followed. Almost all children attended primary school but most left education behind between the ages of 12 and 14 and sought work. Secondary education was the preserve of the wealthy and the academically gifted who could procure scholarships. Those who received an education had a better opportunity of being able to live and work in Ireland and by the turn of the century there was a growing Catholic middle class of doctors, solicitors, civil servants and teachers. The majority were still poor, however. Some 15 per cent of Galway's population were illiterate in 1911, the second highest of any county in Ireland. In the same year, the county had nearly 35,000 housing units, some 400 of which were described as 'perishable' and of the poorest type.

A young girl in Maam Valley (1913), helping with the turf (from *The Charm of Ireland* by Burton Egbert Stevenson).

On the other end of the scale, nearly 2,000 houses in Co. Galway had more than ten rooms. By 1900, there was an undoubted class system in Galway among the former tenants themselves, as described by the author J.M. Synge when speaking of Spiddal:

> I saw people coming from Mass. The police and coastguards came first, dressed like the people of Dublin. Then the well to do country folk, dressed in the local clothes but the best and the newest kind. The wearers themselves looked well-fed and healthy. Then last of all, the destitute in still the same clothes but this time patched and ragged, the women mostly barefooted and both sexes pinched with hunger. [14]

Despite the huge levels of emigration, there had undoubtedly been improvements in the lives of the people of Galway in the two decades before 1900. By the turn of the century, bigger and better-built houses, as well as sheds and outhouses, were becoming increasingly common. Farm animals no longer commonly shared the home with the family in the winter months. In 1903, the British government introduced the Wyndham Act, which helped advance loans to tenant farmers to buy out their plots of land. Although they would have to pay these loans off for years, this was truly transformative and thousands of Galway families took up the scheme, marking the beginning of the end for the landed families who had ruled over Galway for centuries.

14 Synge, J.M. (1911), *In Wicklow, West Kerry and Connemara*, p.102.

FURTHER OPPORTUNITIES FOR GALWAY

There were a small number of opportunities outside agriculture in Galway in the early 1900s and rapid progress was made in some areas using modern technology. The railway was one example. A trainline from Dublin to Galway had been opened in 1851. Someone leaving Galway City could now be in Dublin in a matter of hours and in relative comfort, with stops at major towns such as Athenry and Ballinasloe, benefitting these areas and their hinterland. The railway also opened Galway up to tourists from the rest of Ireland and Britain, the region being widely advertised in England and beyond in the Victorian Age. Galway City, which maintained its quaint and medieval character, was now easily accessed and began to attract flocks of tourists. Connemara, untamed and dotted with mountains and lakes for hikers and fishermen, also proved popular.

The trip to Connemara was more difficult, however. After arriving to Galway, other than walking, the only option of getting to Connemara was on the Bianconi Car, a horse-drawn passenger vehicle that was not renowned for its comfort. One German writer, Julius Rodenberg, embarked on a tour of Connemara for his book *The Harp of Erin*. He was less than impressed with the transport, needing to wrap himself in a plaid blanket to withstand the bitter cold. He stated that his legs, dangling off the edge, quickly became caked in mud, while all passengers were forced to disembark and walk up any hills. He also recounted how he was enveloped in tobacco smoke, while a fellow passenger's hat got blown off and he had to run over half a mile to retrieve it! Other railway lines were built in Galway after the original line. In fact, by the turn of the century, towns such as Tuam, Gort and Loughrea were all connected on the network. The line to Clifden finally opened in 1895, giving

A fisherman in Galway (from *One Irish Summer* by William Curtis).

tourists a new route to the tourist capital of the county, and hotels popped up along it, including at Recess. The seaside resort of Salthill was also connected to Galway City by a tram by 1900 and became popular among the county's elite.

The power of the railway would gradually begin to wane after the importation of Ireland's first motor car in 1898. This amazing horseless carriage, invented in Germany the previous decade, might have seemed like a futuristic fad, and as late as 1904 there were only thirty-eight cars registered in Ireland, the roads being crater-filled and narrow. Nevertheless, the number grew exponentially to more than 5,000 by the night of the 1911 census and it is notable that many of the hotels and landed families in Galway declared motor garages as part of their property in that year's census. Cars were beyond the wildest dreams of ordinary people, however, and boats remained a common means of transport for those living beside the water. In Connemara, *currachs*, often called canoes locally, were used to traverse the peninsulas and islands dotting the coast, while those living along the shores of Lough Corrib also utilised boats for fishing, transportation and leisure.

Galway also did its best to make the most of its natural resources and mining operations were proving to be big business, including at Shantalla where both marble and granite were in abundant supply. There were huge deposits of marble at Recess in Connemara also, while rumours swirled of other materials such as molybdenite at Murvey, near Roundstone, and silica at Letter Hill. The area around Ballinasloe town was famous for its limestone quarries, the stone exported from the town to New York to carve a street of shopfronts in the city. The port at Galway was also intermittently successful, although never to the extent of Queenstown (later Cobh) in Co. Cork, which welcomed *Titanic* on its doomed maiden journey in 1912. The hope in Galway that the port could become the foremost transatlantic port in Europe never materialised, although it still provided employment opportunities in the city. Another good news story economically in the county at this time was the building of the Marconi Station just outside Clifden, which was the first of its kind in the world. The station was capable of telegraphing messages to Glace Bay in Nova Scotia and the first commercial transatlantic message was sent in 1907. The station proved to be a strong employer in the impoverished region of Connemara and messages across the ocean continued to be exchanged for a decade and a half.

By 1911, the most popular surnames in County Galway were Kelly, Walsh, Burke, Conneely, Joyce, Flaherty, Mannion, Keane, Fahy and Murphy. All of these maintain a strong presence in the county today. Galway had other less common surnames, of course. Barnacle was a surname shared by just two families in Co. Galway in 1911, although one of their number, Nora from Bowling Green in the city, went on to become one of the county's most famous people, marrying James Joyce and becoming a muse for many of his most famous characters. Interestingly, there were also several first names that were almost unique to areas of Co. Galway, usually named after local saints. Iomar, for example, was and remains a common name in parts of east Galway, while Jarlath is exceptionally popular in the north of the county. In Connemara, Colman, Caillín and Feichín are names popular in different areas that are uncommon elsewhere.

POLITICAL CHANGE IN GALWAY

In 1898, the Local Government Act changed County Galway's boundaries, which had been in place for hundreds of years, and the large county ceded several rural areas that had close links with towns in neighbouring counties. This included the area around Finny in north Connemara, around thirty townlands in total, which were moved into Co. Mayo. The area around the village of Creggs in the north-east of the county was transferred to Roscommon, while the village of Mountshannon was ceded to Clare. A small portion of Ballinasloe in Co. Roscommon was granted to Galway in return. This act had another function that changed Ireland forever. It ended landlord control of local government and replaced the former grand juries and boards of guardians with directly elected county councils. With increasing numbers of ordinary people enfranchised to vote, this shortly led to most of the representatives on Galway County Council being in favour of Home Rule. Galway's relationship with Britain was complicated, as illustrated by King Edward's visit to the county in 1903. His reception was mixed – Galway County Council had a nationalist majority and decided to ignore the royal visit, while the City Council agreed to take part in the celebrations. In parts of

Connemara, such as Tullycross, there were small crowds to greet the royal party, although many locals snubbed the monarch and refused to turn up. Opinion in the city was also mixed, although Galway City Council ensured that the main thoroughfares were festooned with Union flags. There were also many advertisements in local newspapers from residents of the city renting out their windows to anyone who wanted a good view of the king's cavalcade.

Politically, Ireland was in a state of flux in the first decades of the twentieth century. The working classes in the town were demanding change and there were numerous strikes in Galway between 1910 and 1913, the city having a well-organised trade council. The movement to secure the vote for women was also gathering speed in Ireland and Galway was one of the first counties to embrace the suffragette movement. One of the most prominent of its members was Florence Moon. Originally from Birmingham, Florence had married Charles Moon, a well-known businessman in the city. She quickly devoted herself to local causes and in 1911 was among a crowd who gathered to listen to the well-known suffragette Christabel Pankhurst in Galway Town Hall. Two years later, Moon co-founded the Connacht Women's Franchise League, which aimed to secure the vote for women in Ireland. She was a prolific letter writer on behalf of the women of her adopted home. Many of these letters stated that allowing women to vote would not only improve the quality of women's lives but also the quality of life in Ireland generally. Thanks to women such as Moon, some Irish women eventually got the vote in 1918, with universal franchise finally extended in 1922.

The Land Acts that were introduced between 1881 and 1903 had been designed to placate the Irish population who were hungry for Home Rule. They had improved matters somewhat for small farmers but many landlords retained ownership of large grazing farms. These fertile grasslands were rented out in large tracts to big farmers and shopkeepers, who fattened their cattle there before selling them on. Protests against such farms and their graziers were commonplace throughout the county. Huge demonstrations occurred regularly, including at Muckloon near Ballygar in December 1908, when thousands of people, together with a pipe band, gathered at a grazing farm and drove the livestock off it. There also remained those in Galway willing to use violence to achieve their political and agrarian aims. In 1909, a constable of the Royal Irish Constabulary (RIC) named Martin Goldrick, who had been accompanying bailiffs carrying out an eviction, was shot dead near Craughwell. Two members of the secretive Irish Republican Brotherhood (IRB) movement were later charged with the murder but acquitted.

Although Galway voted overwhelmingly for the Irish Parliamentary Party, which sought to secure Home Rule peacefully, a movement named Sinn Féin had been founded in 1905 by Edward Martyn of Tulira Castle, Ardrahan. Martyn had long been a supporter of the Irish language and had financed many plays and concerts dedicated to national culture. The party's aim was to secure full independence and it would go on to play a huge role in the transformation of Ireland, but it had to wait more than a decade to achieve popular support. In 1913, another organisation called the Irish Volunteers was set up in Dublin. The Volunteers' aim was to unapologetically agitate for self-determination and they wasted little time in founding a branch in Galway. The opening meeting in the city was attended by three well-known Republicans: Eoin McNeill, Roger Casement and Pádraig Pearse, the latter two having strong links to Galway. Hundreds of men joined the organisation in Galway on that first evening and, within weeks, branches were being formed all over their county and drilling commenced in fields, on beaches and in the street. By July 1914, there were nearly 6,000 volunteers in Co. Galway alone, demanding the long-awaited parliament in Dublin to be sanctioned. The next decade was to change Ireland forever.

8

GALWAY'S FIGHT FOR INDEPENDENCE

FIRST WORLD WAR AND GALWAY

The First World War was to transform Irish life and politics. The war, declared in August 1914, pitted Britain, France and Russia against Germany and her allies. John Redmond, the foremost Home Rule politician at the time, urged Irishmen to enlist in the British Army, assuring them that the grateful British administration was sure to grant the long-awaited Home Rule after the war, which the authorities confidently predicted would be over by Christmas. Many enlisted, but the Irish Volunteers were split, some believing that Irishmen had no stake in what they considered Britain's war. More than 12,000 ultimately repudiated Redmond's remarks but Galway City showed strong support for the war effort. It had long been a garrison town with British soldiers stationed there, something that provided economic benefits and rendered the city somewhat less nationalistic in its outlook than the rural areas around it. Recruitment drives in the city were buoyant. In fact, the city was described derisively in 1914 by volunteer Thomas Courtney as 'the most *shoneen* town in Ireland'.

A scene from the First World War (from *True Stories of the Great War* by Francis Trevelyan Miller).

Thousands of Galway men served in the British armed forces and around 1,200 of them from all over the county are thought to have lost their lives in the trenches of Europe between 1914 and 1918. Volunteers also had a strong presence in County Galway, however. Open drilling by their members continued in the early days of the global conflict and anti-war sentiment hardened on hearing of the mounting casualties in Europe. Posters urging Irishmen not to become cannon fodder for the British Army were placed all over Co. Galway. The British administration tried to ignore the Volunteer movement, deriding it as an irrelevance due to its lack of support. The east of the county had a long history of subversion and militant nationalism, however, and was a particular stronghold for the group. In March 1915, Wexford native Liam Mellows was dispatched to east Galway to organise the Irish Volunteers in the area. He worked tirelessly, and interest in the movement continued to grow. When the Easter Rising of 1916 commenced, east Galway was one of a tiny number of areas outside of Dublin that saw meaningful action.

THE EASTER RISING

The Easter Rising was masterminded by a small inner circle of nationalists, known as the Irish Republican Brotherhood. Pádraig Pearse was a central figure. He believed that a strike for freedom should be taken while the British were fighting on the Continent. Although he was aware that such a rebellion would have little prospect of success, Pearse believed that it would propel ordinary Irish people into action. Seven men signed the Proclamation of the Irish Republic, which declared Irish freedom and promised equal rights for all its citizens. One of them was Éamonn Ceannt. Born in the north-eastern Galway village of Ballymoe in 1881, Ceannt was the son of an RIC officer and his family moved around regularly during his childhood on account of his father's profession. Ultimately, Ceannt received much of his schooling in Dublin, where he was known as a keen sportsman and musician. He fell in love with Irish language and culture and quickly rose through the ranks of the Gaelic League, eventually becoming a teacher of the language. He also travelled through rural Ireland, especially Galway, collecting airs for the uilleann pipes, which at the time were being played by an decreasing number of people. When the Irish Volunteers were formed in 1913, he joined up, and later came to be a pivotal figure in the Brotherhood.

Plans for the Rising to go ahead on Easter Sunday, 1916, were scuppered by the detection of a shipment of arms arriving off the coast of Kerry. Poorly armed though they were, it was decided that the operations would still go ahead, although a day late, on Easter Monday, 24 April, 1916. Several of Dublin's most prominent buildings were seized that morning, much to the shock of the authorities. A siege and bombardment from British soldiers and gunboats, lasting six days, soon began. Communication was cut off from the capital to the rest of Ireland and although the Easter Rising centred mainly around Dublin City, unbeknownst to the leaders Galway had also risen, seeing more mobilisations than any other county. Liam Mellows and his fellow conspirators had planned to take over several buildings in Galway city centre, while simultaneously attacking RIC barracks in the vicinity and interfering with post offices and railway stations to impede communication in and out of the city.

They struck on Tuesday, one day after events in Dublin, attacking barracks at Clarinbridge and Oranmore. Neither of these attacks was successful, but fearing mass unrest, martial law was declared in Galway by the authorities and the security of important buildings was reinforced. There was only one fatality in Galway as a direct result of the Rising. Patrick Whelan, a young RIC constable, was shot dead at an ambush near Carnmore. The rebels ultimately ended up at Moyode Castle near Athenry, where they heard the news of the arrival of a British warship in Galway Bay. That caused hundreds of citizens living beside the sea to flee inland in terror. The rebels stayed at Moyode for several days but there were no further engagements. Anticlimactically, they dispersed on Saturday morning, many leaders, including Liam Mellows, going on the run.

The Rising had been disapproved of by many Irish people initially – thousands of Irishmen were fighting in the trenches in the First World War and attempting a rebellion in Ireland seemed to many a dangerous folly. In many cases the 1916 leaders were jeered and spat at by the people after their arrest. Sixteen leaders of the Rising were ultimately executed for their part in what Britain considered a treasonous rebellion, while, in its own words, the British Empire 'fought for small nations' abroad. Éamonn Ceannt, who had been commander of the South Dublin Union during the conflict, was court-martialled and found guilty as one of the Rising's instigators. He was ultimately shot by firing squad on 8 May 1916 and buried in Arbour Hill Prison. He left behind his wife, Áine Brennan, and one son, Ronan. The executions, and the barbaric treatment of the rebels by the British, including tying a mortally wounded James Connolly to a chair and shooting him dead, proved highly controversial and as the body count mounted, Britain found that Irish public opinion rapidly began to change, many criticising the British for their lack of mercy.

The mindset of the people of Galway underwent a rapid transformation. The city council initially passed a motion condemning the Rising, but within a year most of its members were publicly on the side of the movement for independence. The people were horrified by the executions of the leaders of the Rising, many of whom had close connections with Galway. Thomas McDonagh and Joseph Plunkett had spent several months on the Aran Islands learning Irish, while Pádraig Pearse owned a cottage in Rosmuc and often spent several months a year there. Roger Casement, hanged for treason for importing arms for the rebels, was also a regular visitor to Connemara, where he worked to alleviate the poverty of the people. Éamonn de Valera, a leader who narrowly escaped the death penalty, was also well known in Galway, having taught Irish between 1911 and 1913 on Tawin Island near Oranmore. Other less well-known Galway natives played an important role in the Easter Rising, including Eva O'Flaherty. Born into a wealthy family near Caherlistrane, Eva was an early convert to nationalism and joined Cumann na mBan, the sister organisation of the Irish Volunteers, on its formation. O'Flaherty acted as a courier between the various occupied buildings in Dublin during the Easter Rising and was recognised for her bravery. De Valera and many other prominent nationalists attended her funeral in the 1960s, showing the esteem in which she was held.

There were more than 300 imprisonments of Galway natives in the aftermath of the Rising, some being dispatched to prison in England and Wales. These jails included the infamous Frongoch in Wales, which came to be known as the University of Revolution due to the close links it established between Republicans from all over the country. Many spent up to a year in this camp but on their release returned to Galway with new contacts and ideas on how to secure independence. Support for Sinn Féin, the political arm of the IRB, had been negligible before 1916 but grew exponentially in the aftermath of the Rising. William King, a native of Leenane and member of the Irish Republican Army (IRA) in the years after the Rising, talked of the profound effect event had on his teenage psyche: 'I thought of those strange men who dared to attack the great British Empire. I felt a funny feeling deep down in my stomach, and I could not stop the tears coming into my eyes.'[15]

The change in attitude took time, however. As late as 1917, the *Galway Observer* was still lambasting Sinn Féin, who it said was made up of traitors and former graziers. Seamus O'Malley, a United Irish League organiser, said at a meeting in Connemara:

> Who are these pure blind Sinn Fein idiots? They are men and women without the courage to procure for themselves the grazing farms. They were conspicuous on the day when the cattle drives took place. They hid in a ditch. Give up your foolish talk of an Irish republic. Your ambition shall never be realised to win Ireland by physical force from the British Empire.[16]

15 BMH – *Witness Statement, William King.*
16 *Galway Observer*, 30 March 1918.

The people of Galway had already begun to see full independence as something worth fighting for, however, and within a few short years, O'Malley would be proven very wrong.

A WAR IN GALWAY LOOMS

A further turning point came in April 1918 when the British parliament elected to introduce conscription to Ireland. With mounting casualties, the British Army needed a new source of recruits and it was decided that Irishmen should be forcibly enlisted. This proved wildly unpopular and massive protests against the move were held all over Galway. Seven thousand people attended a rally in Tuam on 14 April, showing their vehement opposition to the proposed bill and insisting that they would not be forced into fighting another country's war. The Catholic bishops in Galway were also openly against the move, while the United Irish League condemned it as an attempt to gain cannon fodder for the depleted British Army. Such opposition ensured that conscription in Ireland never came to pass. The British were alarmed by the rapid changes in the mindset of the Irish people and many blamed the country's growing cultural nationalism. In 1918 attempts were made to suppress Irish cultural activities, such as the Gaelic Athletic Association (GAA). The organisation was informed that governmental permission would from then on be needed before any matches could be held. On 27 July, for example, several camogie matches were proclaimed for not having permits, including Gurteen vs Skehana, while a football match between Tuam and Cortoon met the same fate. A day of mass disobedience, Gaelic Sunday, was organised for 4 August 1918, when hundreds of Gaelic football and hurling matches were held simultaneously.

Many of these matches were in Galway, including at South Park in the city where two matches went ahead unimpeded. The GAA reasoned that there was no way the authorities could suppress every game. They were proven right and the British government had to admit defeat.

The First World War came to an end in November 1918. Many people in Galway had supported the war effort initially but enthusiasm had largely dissipated by the conflict's end. The Protestant community of Galway had provided many soldiers to the British forces and generally remained loyal. One member of Galway's tiny Presbyterian Community, 18-year-old Frances Moffett, wished to celebrate the British victory. She received a wholly negative reaction on the streets of Galway when attempting to do so:

> I went into a shop on my way home. 'Can I have a yard of red, white and blue ribbon?' I asked. 'I'll not sell any such thing,' said the shop assistant, to my amazement. I eventually got the ribbon in a bigger shop and displayed a long bow in celebration on my bicycle before I began the mile-long journey home. [At Bohermore] I found myself soaked with a bucket of dirty suds. A woman shouted 'Take that, you orange dog.' I stood still and looked at my soaked skirt. Then I looked at the woman standing in her cottage doorway, the bucket still swinging in her hand. She was muttering something – I caught 'The damned British' and 'My Paddy tortured in prison'.[17]

A general election was called for December 1918, with Sinn Féin running on a platform demanding full independence. Galway was divided into four constituencies and Sinn Féin won them all convincingly. Irish-language activist Pádraig Ó Máille romped home in Connemara, hammering William

17 Moffet, F. (1985), *I Also Am of Ireland*, p.91.

O'Malley of the Irish Parliamentary Party who had been a sitting politician for more than two decades. O'Malley blamed his defeat on the GAA and Irish dancing clubs, which he said were politicising the youth of Connemara. Liam Mellows was not even in Ireland for the election but was nevertheless returned unopposed for Galway East. Dr Bryan Cusack was another Sinn Féin candidate popular with the grassroots and he too got elected easily. South Galway was no different and Frank Fahy, a veteran of the Rising, was elected with nearly six times as many votes as his rival from the IPP. The results mirrored the rest of the country, bar the north-east, which retained its unionist majority. It was clear that Galway, and Ireland, had changed utterly and Home Rule was no longer sufficient. Full independence was the goal. All the elected Sinn Féin members refused to attend Westminster, instead going to the Mansion House in Dublin where the Dáil, the new Irish parliament, was convened on 21 January 1919 despite most of its elected representatives being missing due to being locked up or on the run. They pronounced themselves the rightful rulers of the island of Ireland. Éamonn de Valera was elected president, seconded by Galway TD Pádraig Ó Máille. On the same day, two RIC policemen who were transporting gelignite were shot dead by IRA volunteers. The War of Independence had begun.

THE WAR OF INDEPENDENCE

Galway eventually became the scene of much death and destruction but the first months of 1919 were quiet. In fact, there was much more concern about the Spanish Flu that was claiming thousands of lives throughout Ireland. North Galway was badly hit and fever hospitals there were seeing ten deaths a week at the height of the spread, the *Tuam Herald* reporting that several children were made orphans with both their parents dying in the pandemic. There was a low level of violence against government targets, but this was confined mainly to southern counties. Galway appeared calm. In April, however, the Dáil announced a boycott of the RIC. The people of the county were warned by the Republican movement that they were no longer to deal with policemen who, as the eyes and ears of the British government, were the enemies of the people. Instead, the newly formed Irish Republican Police were tasked with dealing with any crime. People were instructed to ignore the British justice system and were forbidden from giving evidence or acting as jurors. Within months, it was on the brink of collapse. Instead, Dáil courts were set up, with Republicans acting as arbitrators on local criminal behaviour and legal disputes. The British government remained steadfast in their aim of maintaining control and not dealing with Sinn Féin, however, and conflict appeared imminent.

Violence was still uncommon in Galway as 1920 dawned, although by this stage there were many land disputes ongoing. Any landlord who owned grazing land was facing increasing intimidation. On the Ross estate in March 1920, for example, a 200-strong crowd, mainly tenants of the estate itself, called at the residences of large graziers, telling those within to vacate their land immediately. In others cases, graziers were attacked, threatened and sent intimidating notices. Cattle driving also remained a common tactic. By now, there were killings on a regular basis nationally and it seemed only a matter of time until fatal violence came to Galway. On 3 March 1920, Frank Shawe-Taylor, an unpopular land agent who had refused to allow his large farm to be divided, was shot dead near Athenry. Just two days later, John Heanue, a policeman and native of Tullycross, Co. Galway, was shot dead at a shop near the Ragg, Co. Tipperary. The war had arrived to the west and police, land agents and ultimately British soldiers drafted into the country found themselves on the front line of a conflict few foresaw just three years before.

By spring 1920, the situation was rapidly getting out of control in the eyes of the government. Killings of RIC officers were mounting and the police began to abandon smaller rural barracks for better-fortified stations in the towns of Galway. Soon, the vast expanse of west Connemara had just two police stations remaining, at Clifden and Maam, down from more than a dozen in 1919. East Galway villages also found that RIC officers formerly stationed there had been moved into towns such as Loughrea, Tuam and Ballinasloe. The IRA now had control over rural Galway and, in the first week of April, orders were given to local units to burn as many abandoned police barracks as possible so that they could not be reoccupied. The Galway IRA took up this task with gusto, destroying stations all over the county; from Barnaderg, to Moycullen, to Letterfrack and elsewhere.

THE BLACK AND TANS

The RIC was by now losing members through resignations, deaths in ambushes and even suicides. Consequently, the authorities decided to recruit ex-British army reinforcements to shore up the depleted force. Within a year, there were a staggering 50,000 British troops based in Ireland. The new recruits were divided between the Auxiliaries, a smaller paramilitary police force of ex-army officers, and a larger group of ordinary ex-soldiers, who became known as the Black and Tans due to the colour of their hastily gathered and mismatched uniforms. The latter would become synonymous with violent reprisals and indiscriminate attacks and grow to be hated by most of the population of Co. Galway. IRA veteran Colm Ó Gaora had many dealings with the Black and Tans in Co. Galway and later wrote scathingly of them:

> The British sent the Black and Tans into the area as a form of back-up to the local police. The raggle-taggle militia that was the Tans was composed of two types. The 'lowlifes' of British society, murderers and rapists who would have spent their lives behind bars if the British government hadn't set them loose on the Irish people … and former British soldiers who were unemployed now that the First World War was over and who were well trained in both guerrilla tactics and the use of weapons. It was hard to know which of these two elements were worse.[18]

The Black and Tans were indeed ruthless. Any act of IRA violence was met with a vicious and indiscriminate reprisal in the local area. On 19 July 1920, IRA volunteers ambushed RIC officers on the road between Tuam and Dunmore, killing two of the officers but allowing the other two to surrender once they had handed over their arms. Unable to find the ambushers, the enraged Black and Tans stationed in the locality went on a rampage that evening and burned down several buildings in Tuam. Such acts of destruction would become their calling card nationally in the months to come. On 21 August 1920 another RIC officer was killed when a patrol was ambushed close to Merlin Park in Galway City. On this occasion nearby Oranmore was sacked in reprisal.

The city experienced a night of terror on 8 September 1920 when IRA volunteer Sean Mulvoy was shot dead at Galway Railway Station when he attempted to disarm an

18 O' Gaora, C. (2011), *On the Run*, p.137.

errant Black and Tan, Edward Krumm. Krumm was also shot dead in the struggle. The Black and Tans avenged their colleague's death by shooting Republican Seamus Quirke dead in the city, burning buildings and sacking the offices of the *Galway Express* newspaper, known for its Republican sympathies. Excesses such as these were beginning to make international headlines and the British, while publicly backing the Black and Tans, were in private worried about their violent actions. Any lingering support for British rule in Galway was extinguished by several deplorable events in the county in October and November 1920, the two bloodiest months in Galway's modern history. It began on 19 October, when a Sinn Féin councillor named Michael Walsh was forcibly taken from the Old Malt Pub in Galway City and shot dead several hundred metres away on the Long Walk, his body dumped in the River Corrib.

Two weeks later, on 1 November, Eileen Quinn, a pregnant young mother, was holding one of her children by the side of the road at Kiltartan near Gort when a lorry

The Spanish Arch as pictured in 1909. Michael Walsh's body was dumped from the Long Walk, seen in the top right of the picture (from *One Irish Summer* by William Eleroy Curtis).

load of Black and Tans passed by. They were firing randomly into bushes, as they often did to deter potential IRA ambush parties, when Eileen was hit with a stray bullet. It took her several hours to bleed to death and the murder and subsequent cover-up, which concluded that the killing was a 'death by misadventure', caused outrage in Galway. A further incident that horrified the local population occurred at around midnight on 14 November 1920, when three men called at the house of Fr Michael Griffin on Montpellier Terrace to the west of Galway City. They claimed to want the popular priest to come on an urgent sick call. He obliged but was not seen alive again. Fr Griffin's body was discovered days later buried in a shallow grave some miles west near Barna. Although Griffin had Republican sympathies, he was not outspoken in his views and the brutal murder of a man of the cloth was a shocking affair, his funeral attracting more than 10,000 mourners. A military whitewash inquiry declared that Griffin had been shot by persons unknown, although the Bishop of Galway himself publicly stated that he believed the British forces had been complicit in the murder and subsequent cover-up. Subsequent evidence from British troops themselves indicate that the unfortunate priest was shot at Lenaboy Castle in Salthill before being buried in secret. The British denied responsibility. The killing may have been in retaliation for the IRA execution of Patrick Joyce a month earlier. Joyce was a Galway schoolteacher who had been taken from his home and tried by an IRA delegation in an abandoned house near Moycullen. He was found guilty of sending letters with incriminating evidence against IRA volunteers to the British government, shot and secretly buried. Fr Griffin was among those named in a letter from Joyce to government forces as a Republican sympathiser and this could be why he was chosen.

FURTHER VIOLENCE IN GALWAY

Galway was already reeling from these terrible events when, on 26 November, an even more gruesome killing was carried out by British forces. On this occasion, a patrol of auxiliaries was driving around the Gort area looking for anyone known to be involved with the IRA. Their plan was to gain revenge for an ambush a month earlier on police in Castledaly, several miles away, where a policeman was killed. Brothers Patrick and Harry Loughnane were threshing hay with several neighbours and a steam-powered machine and they did not hear the approach of the lorry with about fifteen officers on board. They were surrounded, captured and taken away before being interrogated and eventually killed by Crown Forces near Ardrahan. Their frantic mother visited several police stations looking for them, the British insisting that they had escaped from custody and they knew nothing of the Loughnanes' whereabouts. It transpired that the pair, who were members of the local IRA, had been tortured and killed, their bodies dumped in a pool of water and covered in oil to hamper detection and identification. A decision by a local teacher, Tomás Ó hEighin, to take pictures of the mutilated corpses and distribute them, would give us arguably the most sickening image of the whole War of Independence and ensure that the story of the Loughnane Brothers remains a source of anger to this day. As ever, no one was prosecuted and the British government of the day showed little interest in pursuing the case. By now, most of the people of Galway were firmly on the side of the IRA and rural areas of the county were totally under Republican control, becoming virtual no-go areas for British troops except in large armoured convoys. Even these occasional raids were unpopular, with good reason. On 18 December 1920, the Crown Forces raided Inishmore, one of the Aran Islands, which had been totally without police for some months. On this raid, they shot dead an unarmed civilian named Laurence McDonagh.

Nationally Ireland was in turmoil, and just before Christmas 1920 the island was officially partitioned. Six counties in the north-east, with an overall unionist majority, were named Northern Ireland and given their own parliament as part of the United Kingdom. One of the driving forces of partition was Edward Carson, a loyalist who refused to countenance being ruled from Dublin. Carson's mother was of the Lambert family from Athenry, Co. Galway, and Edward himself spent many holidays in Galway as a young boy, although they clearly never changed his political allegiance. The remaining twenty-six counties remained at war. The IRA's primary tactic was not to engage in pitched battles against their better-armed and more numerous opponents. Instead, guerilla warfare was the chosen method and by early 1921, the IRA in Galway had formed itself into several brigades, each of which had a flying column containing their elite soldiers. As the war intensified, they went permanently on the run to avoid arrest and murder at the hands of the British. They hid out in barns, on mountainsides and in forests, occasionally picking locations carefully and awaiting British convoys, using the element of surprise to attack their better-armed opponents. If victorious, they took any arms available and melted back into the surrounding countryside. This proved a highly successful tactic and the infuriated Crown Forces continued to take their anger out on nearby houses and villages, usually of innocent people, further eroding any support for them. Not everyone agreed with the ambush policy of the IRA, however. The Archbishop of Tuam, Thomas Gilmartin, issued a letter stating that IRA volunteers who took part in ambushes were guilty of murder.

Many of his own priests disagreed, however, and gave tacit support to the freedom fighters.

CUMANN NA MBAN IN GALWAY

Women also played an important role in the battle for independence, largely due to their role in Cumann na mBan. Founded in 1914, the nationalist organisation was an auxiliary force of the Irish Volunteers for women and was stronger in Galway than many places nationwide. The county was among the first outside to Dublin to set up a branch. Cumann na mBan had their own military-style uniform and provided any assistance possible to Republicans in their struggle for independence, be this carrying messages, providing safe houses, or importing and concealing weapons. Many women would be imprisoned for these activities, including Bridget Dirrane, a native of the Aran Islands. Bridget met many important revolutionaries in her youth, including Pádraig Pearse, Thomas MacDonagh and Joseph Plunkett, all of whom had come to the island to learn Irish. Bridget joined Cumann na mBan and drilled regularly. She became known to the Black and Tans and was eventually arrested and imprisoned in Mountjoy Prison, going on hunger strike there for a time. She spoke Irish to the guards and spent much of her time Irish dancing while in prison, much to the irritation of her captors.

Alice M. Cashel was another important figure in the movement. She was a senior organiser nationally, as well as a councillor and a Republican judge in Galway. Peg Broderick Nicholson was a third luminary in Galway's Cumann na mBan. Born in Prospect Hill in the city into a family with a strong nationalist outlook, Peg joined the organisation in 1917 and carried out many vital tasks, including carrying dispatches, interrupting British meetings and carrying out intelligence work. She was beaten at one point and at another stage had her hair shaved off by Black and Tans as a punishment.

FURTHER VIOLENCE IN 1921

The Kilroe Ambush was the first major engagement in Galway in 1921 and occurred about 4 miles south-west of Headford on 18 January. The north Galway brigade of the IRA carefully planned the ambush on a party of Auxiliaries, injuring several of them in the process. This was followed by vicious Black and Tan reprisals in north Galway over several days, with four local men being taken from their houses and shot. Two policemen, Charles Reynolds and Thomas Sweeney, were shot dead by the IRA while on patrol in Clifden, Co. Galway, two months later on 16 March 1921. These shootings were as a reprisal for the execution in Dublin of Clifden native Thomas Whelan. Whelan had been implicated in shooting a British officer in the capital on Bloody Sunday in November 1920, something that he vehemently denied and which was contradicted by numerous eyewitnesses. Nevertheless, he was hanged and the policemen were shot two days later. Like Tuam before it, Clifden was burned in response and one innocent local man, John McDonnell, was shot dead by a group of Black and Tans who arrived in the town by train.

The IRA column in Connemara had by now retreated into the mountains and would shortly stage other ambushes, first at Screebe near Rosmuc, where one policeman was critically injured, and then at Munterowen near Maam on 23 April, when another policeman was shot dead. This flying column was particularly successful in avoiding detection. Aeroplanes, then in their infancy, were even used by the British to try

The Twelve Bens Mountains, which shielded the IRA (from *Connaught* by Stephen Gwynn).

and locate the volunteers but these proved unsuccessful, the volunteers being able to use the Maamturk and Twelve Bens mountains to shield themselves.

The deaths also continued in the rest of County Galway. Christopher and Joseph Folan were shot dead by Black and Tans in a house search in May in Galway City. They later shot Hubert Tully, a suspected Republican. The IRA also continued their activity, although they were increasingly short of weaponry. On 15 May 1921, the south-west Galway IRA brigade ambushed a car as it departed from the home of the Gregory family, Ballyturin House, near Gort. Four of the occupants, two army officers and a policeman and his wife, were killed. The RIC were quickly on the scene, one of their number also being shot dead as he arrived. This was one of the deadliest attacks in the War of Independence in the west and the deaths were a hammer blow to British forces in the area. In reprisal, police burned several houses on the road from the ambush site to Gort.

The people of Galway had grown weary of the terrible struggle and there was widespread relief on 9 July 1921 when it was announced that a truce was to take effect two days later. The IRA in Galway kept going until the truce took hold, however, and on the evening of 10 July two off-duty RAF men were taken prisoner by local IRA men when they were drinking in a pub with their girlfriends in Oranmore. The airmen were ultimately released unharmed on the morning of 11 July, however, after the Truce came into effect. A final incident occurred on the morning of 11 July when local IRA volunteers ambushed an RIC patrol near Kilchreest in south Galway. There were no fatalities and the truce held. The people of Galway could breathe a sigh of relief. Briefly, as it turned out.

THE TRUCE

The Truce meant that IRA men on the run could return to their homes and that police and soldiers could feel more confident of going about their business unimpeded. Curfews, which had been in place for ordinary civilians, were also lifted. Nevertheless, there was a wariness that talks could break down and that hostilities would restart. The IRA continued to drill and train and received thousands of new recruits, later derisively called 'Trucileers'. The Truce saw a seven-man Irish delegation being chosen to travel to London to negotiate. They were led by Michael Collins and Arthur Griffith and after exhaustive talks they agreed to sign the Anglo-Irish Treaty. This document acknowledged the partition of Ireland. In return, Ireland would get its own parliament in Dublin in charge of its own internal affairs, although one where members would be obliged to swear an oath of allegiance to the King of England. This new entity would be called the Irish Free State and, although it would fall short of the republic many had fought for, the delegation narrowly backed it, believing it was a stepping stone to full freedom.

The deal was hugely controversial and many Republicans regarded it as a betrayal of what their comrades had fought for. The Dáil, however, backed the Treaty narrowly, sixty-four votes to fifty-seven. Galway members George Nicolls, Joseph Whelehan, Patrick Hogan and Pádraig Ó Máille voted in favour; Liam Mellows, Bryan Cusack, Frank Fahy were against, the numbers almost exactly mirroring the national picture. Éamonn de Valera was the leader of Sinn Féin but had inexplicably refused to attend the talks himself. He quickly announced himself bitterly opposed to the Treaty and consequently to his former comrades who had voted for the document. He resigned his post as president when the Treaty was passed and brought many of the IRA with him. Galway had played its role in the fight for independence and, like the rest of the country, was bitterly divided on the Treaty. Many active soldiers from the War of Independence were against the document, while most civilians wished to accept it and return to a life of peace.

On 26 March 1922, 200 IRA delegates met at an army convention, where they announced their opposition to the Treaty and their unwillingness to follow the direction of the Dáil. Less than a month later, on 14 April, Liam Mellows was among 200 anti-Treaty fighters who took over the Four Courts in Dublin in a direct show of defiance against the government. Collins and the pro-Treaty side, reluctant to blunder into a civil war, did nothing at the time and the following month, Collins and de Valera agreed to sign a pact to jointly contest the forthcoming election. On 23 April 1922, de Valera and two other important anti-Treaty figures, Harry Boland and Cathal Brugha, arrived in Galway to speak on the issue of the Treaty. There was a crowd of about 2,000 people, with several prominent Galway natives on the stage, including the brother of Fr Michael Griffin who had been abducted and killed two years before. De Valera asked the assembled crowd:

> Do you think you would destroy that Republic, and set up a monarchy in its place, and go to England for your monarch? You know you would not. If you were independent, would you take over, willingly, a portion of Britain's war debts, and burden yourselves with an annual sum to pay off these debts? No. You know you would not. Therefore, they lie when they say that you have your independence. If you accept this Treaty, you will be putting shackles on your own limbs with your own hands.[19]

There seemed to be little uniting the sides other than a vague agreement that the British were the enemy. On 25 May 1922, a statue of Lord Dunkellin, a former MP from Galway who had been a British Army captain and loyal subject of the Empire, was toppled at Eyre Square. The monument had stood for fifty years but was unceremoniously dragged by the crowds through the streets and thrown into the sea at the Spanish Arch. The pact between the pro- and anti-Treaty sides barely lasted until the election on 16 June, where pro-Treaty candidates won a substantial majority of voters. In the nine-seater Galway constituency, the pro-Treaty Sinn Féin side won 54.5 per cent of the vote, the anti-Treaty side winning just 32.3 per cent. The Labour party, who also advocated accepting the Treaty, took the remainder. The public were, largely, on the side of accepting the Treaty, despite its cementing of the partition of Ireland and its acceptance of an oath of allegiance to the king.

19 *Connacht Tribune*, 29 April 1922.

Relations between the two sides deteriorated rapidly after the election and the kidnapping of pro-Treaty army official J.J. O'Connell in Dublin on 27 June 1922 by anti-treaty IRA was the catalyst that led to the army's attack on the Four Courts and the start of the civil war. Orders were quickly given to bomb the Four Courts. War-weary Ireland faced yet another conflict – this time, brother against brother. It was not long until Galway saw more bloodshed.

THE CIVIL WAR

The National Army quickly captured Dublin and marched south and west, taking much of the country with little fighting. Although County Galway had many Republican sympathisers, Galway City was solidly in favour of the Treaty and the National Army took it on 7 July, although there were several injuries in minor scuffles and Republicans set fire to several barracks they had been overseeing before fleeing. These included Renmore and Eglinton Street in the city. The rest of the county would not be so easily won over, however, as shown when Gerald O'Connor, a National Army soldier, was shot and killed when his convoy was ambushed by the anti-Treaty IRA near Gort on 8 July 1922. He was one of the first Free State casualties. Patrick Greaney of Spiddal, another Free State soldier, was shot dead days later. His funeral was also fired upon by Republicans, one of his comrades being killed and several kidnapped. Despite these setbacks, east and south Galway had come under Free State control by the end of the summer, at least nominally – the town of Tuam fell into state hands on 28 July 1922. A curfew of 11 p.m. was set throughout much of Galway. The wild and mountainous region of Connemara would remain hostile country for some time to come, however, as would rural tracts of north Galway.

Nationally, by the end of July, the cities of Limerick and Waterford had fallen and counties Kerry and Cork were among the last places to be pacified, other than west Galway and Mayo. The IRA knew that isolated and mountainous areas such as Connemara were their best chance of holding on to territory and decided to make access to the region difficult for Free State troops. In early July, several bridges were blown up between Galway and Oughterard, both on the road and the railway line, making the running of trains and motor cars from Galway to Clifden an impossibility. Clifden was captured and the barracks and the workhouse occupied by Republicans. On 15 August, Free State troops finally reached Clifden. Before their arrival, Republicans abandoned the town and burned the Marconi transmitter station. The National Army thus took the last remaining major urban area in the county with little resistance. Connemara and parts of north Galway were placed under martial law. The authorities decreed that anyone found destroying bridges or railways or engaged in looting was to be tried by a military court, where the punishment was likely to be harsh. It had little effect. Bridges, including the Ferry Bridge near Clonbur, Shratloe Bridge near Leenane and Derrydonnell Bridge in Athenry, were blown up after this pronouncement. Dozens of other bridges in the county were also mined to hinder the movement of Free State soldiers.

By the end of summer 1922, the Republicans held little ground but were still encamped in the mountains and other remote locations in small fighting groups. They continued to launch sporadic ambushes on state targets, as on 22 August 1922 when Michael Collins, considered by many as the father of the new state, was shot dead in Co. Cork. Collins had sought a peaceful settlement and his death caused outrage. It amplified the bitterness of the civil war and the government soon passed legislation introducing the death penalty for any anti-Treaty soldier found carrying arms. The Republicans were far from finished in Co. Galway, however, despite being condemned by the Catholic Church as terrorists. On 29 October, the anti-Treaty IRA retook Clifden after a ten-hour gun battle. They later announced that any TD who had voted to grant the government powers to execute anti-Treaty fighters was a target, and on 7 December Galway TD Pádraig Ó Máille, the deputy speaker of the Dáil, was shot by gunmen in Dublin as he set out for the parliament, Leinster House. His fellow pro-Treaty TD, Seán Hales, was killed in the incident. This proved to be a pivotal moment in the war. In retribution, four prominent Republicans were executed by firing squad, among them Liam Mellows, known for his exploits in Galway.

By early 1923, most Republicans in Galway had laid down their weapons. Rather than having done so because they had been persuaded of the benefits of the Free State, most were fearful of the merciless execution policy that continued and which ultimately saw eighty-one mainly rank-and-file Republicans shot by firing squad. No fewer than eight of these executions were in Galway, all taking place in Tuam, and making it one of the worst-affected counties in the government's policy of spreading executions around the country to induce maximum fear. Several other Galway men were executed separately at Athlone. Some Republicans maintained the struggle into 1923 and many large stately homes in Co. Galway that were considered to be owned by those loyal to the new state were burned to the ground, including Castlehackett House, Renvyle House and Roxborough House. By late February, it was clear that the civil war was unwinnable from an anti-Treaty perspective. Nevertheless, IRA chief-of-staff Liam Lynch took the opportunity to issue a statement rejecting the possibility of a truce and military operations continued in Galway, albeit on a lesser scale than previously. On 8 April 1923, a Free State soldier was shot dead after an aborted IRA attack on the barracks in Headford.

There were now thousands of Republicans languishing in overcrowded jails around the country, including hundreds at Galway. The fledgling state had little space to hold such numbers of captives and fourteen prisoners escaped from Galway Gaol in April, cutting through the bars using a hacksaw and jumping 8ft onto blankets thrown below to break their fall. On 10 April, Liam Lynch was shot dead in Co. Tipperary. Frank Aiken was elected IRA Chief-of-Staff in his place and quickly called for an end to IRA military operations, an order that was finally supported by Éamonn de Valera. The final executions of the civil war occurred in County Galway, several days after Aiken's orders to cease fighting. Ardrahan natives and IRA members Michael Murphy and Joseph O'Rourke were executed at Tuam Military Barracks for armed robbery. Although hostilities had ended and no one had been killed in the raid, the execution was carried out. An election shortly after the civil war returned the pro-Treaty side, now known as Cumann na nGaedheal, to power. They took four of Galway's nine seats, compared to three for the Republicans, indicating that Galway was still closely split as regards the Treaty. The people of the Irish Free State could finally live in peace at least, although the bitter legacy of the civil war was evident for some time to come.

9

SOCIAL AND POLITICAL LIFE IN GALWAY IN THE NEW STATE

EDUCATION AND CHANGE IN POST-INDEPENDENCE GALWAY

Independence brought some swift changes, policing foremost among them. The Royal Irish Constabulary, which had served in Ireland since 1836 but whose last years had been mired in death and destruction, was disbanded and replaced with a new unarmed police force, the Civic Guard (An Garda Síochána). This new unarmed force was rolled out across the more peaceful east of Ireland from the summer of 1922 but did not come to Galway until the end of September, the civil war still ongoing. It was not until 1923 that officers were able to take up residence in many of Galway's rural villages. Most citizens accepted the new force as apolitical, although some Republicans, still bitter about the treatment meted out to them by the state during the civil war, regarded the Gardaí as little more than lackeys.

The newly independent state was also determined to promote Irish language and culture. Some changes were ceremonial – the formerly red post boxes were painted green, for example. Some were more far-reaching, including the designation of the teaching of the Irish language as mandatory in primary schools. A Gaeltacht Commission report in 1925 stated that Irish was spoken as a community language in parts of twelve of the twenty-six counties, with Galway having by far the highest number of speakers. The southern coast of the county, from Barna to Cashel, had Irish as the undisputed community language, as did the Joyce Country area around Maam, Cornamona and Clonbur. Parts of Claregalway, Menlo and Annaghdown to the east of Galway City were also considered partially Irish speaking. West Connemara, in the hinterland of Clifden, also had some Irish speakers but, like much of the rest of the country, had lost Irish as its community language.

The new state was determined to arrest this decline and the education system was its primary means of doing so. Many teachers trained in the British system spoke no Irish, however, and were swiftly dispatched to the Gaeltacht to learn the language, while thousands of children and teenagers also began to flock there during the summer, providing a huge boost for the depressed economy of south Connemara. Outside these areas, Galway was largely English speaking by the advent of the new state but the Irish language maintained a strong impact even here, with many Irish words remaining commonly in use. In English-speaking Kilmacduagh in 1937, for example, one child wrote a list of words that were still regularly heard in the speech of the district, despite Irish bring unknown to most inhabitants. These included *neanóg* (nettle), *pleidhce* (messer) and *sugán* (rope). Even to this day throughout Galway, one can hear Irish words like *meas* (respect), *amadán* (fool) or *ciotóg* (left-handed person) being used in conversation by people who do not speak Irish.

The new government attempted to stamp its authority on education and made school attendance compulsory for those between the ages of 6 and 14 in 1926. Along with Irish, children studied reading, writing, arithmetic, history, geography, poetry and music, all with a distinctly Irish flavour. Girls and boys generally attended separate schools in Galway towns, while in the countryside there were hundreds of small schools catering for boys and girls together, although these often had a separate entry for the two sexes. In the late 1920s, the Department of Education introduced the Primary School Certificate examination. In the 1940s, this exam was made compulsory for all children who had reached sixth class. Only a small percentage of children proceeded into post-primary education and as late as 1957 only 10,000 students sat the Leaving Certificate, which marked the end of a pupil's secondary education.

THE ECONOMY IN INDEPENDENT GALWAY

Despite these changes, it quickly became clear after the civil war that economically Ireland was much the same as it had been before independence. This was particularly true of the counties of the western seaboard, where the first government struggled to fulfil the promises of prosperity made during the rebellion. Large repayments to Britain had been agreed in the Treaty, placing a drain on Ireland's limited finances. Prospects were poor. An overwhelmingly agricultural economy left the Irish state unable to provide adequately paid work for the children of the large families, which were still commonplace, as they grew to adulthood. There remained many divisions in rural communities over the redistribution of land after the landlords' exodus, many smaller farmers bitterly disappointed with the plots they were given, which generally allowed for only a subsistence living. Galway farms were usually too small for subdivision and could not provide for all the children as they grew into adulthood. Many of those with limited education had little choice but to leave, either to work in Ireland's cities or more commonly to emigrate to America, England, Australia or wherever else they could afford to travel to or where they had connections. American Wakes, gatherings lamenting the coming emigration of a family member to the United States, most never to return, remained common social occasions in Galway after independence and were tinged with great sadness.

Connemara remained the poorest part of the county. A mini-famine in 1924, combined with a cholera outbreak, convinced many that the policies of the new regime were little better than that which went before. A letter from Dr Irwin of Tully was read out in the Dáil chamber in 1927. It indicated that families in the area were going hungry for

A currach, the traditional fishing boat in Galway, in the early nineteenth century (from *On an Irish Jaunting Car* by Samuel Bayne).

large parts of the year and that reparations from emigrants were the only thing keeping the local economy afloat. Other than farming, there were few other means of earning a living in areas such as these. The selling of kelp, a burnt seaweed used for fertiliser, did provide a small additional source of income to some, as did small-scale fishing.

Fishing was a notoriously precarious living, however. Most fishermen had rudimentary equipment and used only the traditional *currach* boat to protect them from the unpredictable weather in the Atlantic Ocean, which claimed many lives in the various fishing communities in twentieth-century Galway. The Cleggan Bay disaster was the worst maritime disaster in modern Galway history. On 28 October 1927, a sudden hurricane struck the west coast. The sheer unpredictability of the weather front meant that many Connemara fishermen were out at sea and unable to make their way back to shore. Ultimately, forty-five fishermen from the Galway fishing communities of Rossadillisk, near Cleggan, and Inishbofin Island, died. Many bodies were never found. This was just one of countless tragedies at sea, many of which affected the small island communities dotted around the coast. Most of Galway's populated offshore islands struggled to survive in the twentieth century and became depopulated, including Inishark, Inishturbot, Island Eddy and Feenish Island.

East Galway was in a slightly better position, the land being more arable and consequently able to produce more food. In fact, farmers in this region were able to take advantage of the lack of employment in the west of the county in their hiring fairs. These were held in towns such as Athenry, and Connemara men came in their hundreds to be hired by farmers from the fertile east to be chosen to work as labourers, often for the summer months, for accommodation and a small wage. These hired labourers were referred to as 'spalpeens'. The farming communities were industrious and largely grew their own crops, baked their own bread, slaughtered their own animals for meat and often made their own clothes. The little money available was earned by selling excess produce or animals. This was used to purchase items in shops that could not be made at home such as teabags, sugar, tobacco and occasionally a sweet for the children. Rent and rates also usually had to be paid. Holidays were unheard of, although summer visitors returning to Galway from abroad or from the cities was the source of much excitement.

Women, who had played a pivotal role in the Irish revolution, expected the new state to provide them with more opportunities. The state was more conservative than many revolutionaries thought it might be, however, and women rarely worked outside the home. The government actively discouraged this, in fact, and all female civil servants, most notably teachers, from 1932 onwards were obliged to give up their post when they married. On the family farm, the woman of the house was usually responsible for the care of the small livestock, the poultry, pigs and calves. She was also often expected to attend to the vegetable garden and to the growing of fruit. Minding the children and sewing and washing clothes were also usually on the lengthy list of chores. There was no running water or electricity at the time, sanitation was poor and there were few modern conveniences to make the rearing of children easier. In a rural east Galway area like Skehana, childbirth, and the attitude towards new mothers, was different than how we know it today:

In the 1950s home births were normal in the area with the assistance of Nurse Kilcommons. When her Morris Minor was seen in the area, either someone was coming into the world or someone was going out. In the 1960s women were increasingly attending hospital to give birth.

It usually meant that the mother was away for up to a week. On the way home from the hospital, the newborn was brought to the church for baptism. The mother did not attend the baptism but waited in the car outside. When the baptism was over the mother was brought in and put sitting in the seat furthest to the back for a ceremony called Churching. I was told at the time it was a cleansing ceremony. Churching had to be done before the mother was permitted to attend religious ceremonies again. Then the child was taken home and was well able to walk before it saw the light of day again.[20]

Health was another worry common to all areas of the county. Dysentery, polio, typhus and tuberculosis were among the diseases that caused thousands of deaths of people of all ages in Co. Galway. In the case of tuberculosis, known as the captain of the men of death, 5,000 deaths a year nationally was the norm in the 1920s and '30s and a sanitorium was built at Merlin Park near the city to administer to those infected with the deadly disease, most of whom were treated as lepers at the time due to the contagious nature of the illness. Polio, a virus that could cause paralysis and death, also killed thousands and left countless other crippled. By the 1950s, deaths from these diseases had become rare due to an enhanced vaccine programme and better health care. Health minister Dr Noel Browne, who had lost both parents to tuberculosis, was the driver in this improvement and lived much of his life in Inverin, Co. Galway. Most villages in Co. Galway had a doctor, although healthcare was rudimentary. Cod liver oil, castor oil, milk of magnesia, Epsom salts, petroleum jelly, gripe water, Andrews Liver Salts and syrup of figs were commonly found in Galway homes as a cure-all, while prescribed medication was rare.

20 skehana.galwaycommunityheritage.org – Growing up in the 1950s and '60s.

ECONOMIC DEVELOPMENT

There were some improvements in farming in the decades after independence, an era that saw a consolidation in the size of farms, which at independence were often as little as 10 acres. By the mid-1950s, however, 45 per cent of farms were in the range of 30 to 100 acres. One of the architects of this improvement was Galway man Patrick Hogan. Born near Killreekil in Co. Galway in 1891, Hogan was a nationalist who was imprisoned in Ballykinlar Camp during the War of Independence. He was an enthusiastic supporter of the Treaty and was appointed minister for agriculture in the Free State government. He was relatively successful in his ministry in difficult economic times and worked hard to consolidate small farms, improve Irish produce and breeding and to raise the number of exports of Irish livestock and crops. He was an impressive public speaker and was regularly elected in a landslide until 1936, when he died in a car accident near Aughrim, Co. Galway, not far from his home. On hearing of his death, former leader of the country W.T. Cosgrave commented, 'Our best man is gone.'

The building of a large sugar factory in Tuam in 1933 was a huge boost to the people of the town and to thousands of farmers of north Galway and further afield. Another potential opportunity for Galway was its location for the burgeoning air travel industry. In 1919, John Alcock and Arthur Whitten Brown became the first pilots to fly the Atlantic Ocean, crash-landing in a bog near Ballyconneely, Co. Galway. The landing was probably the foremost global news event in Galway history and reporters from all over the world descended on the site to meet the flying pioneers who battled freezing fog, technical issues and inclement weather during the sixteen-hour flight. The landing also underlined Galway's potential aeronautical benefits. Longer flights over the following decade meant that regular scheduled Atlantic crossings no longer seemed fanciful by the end of the 1920s and locations on the west coast of Ireland, as the nearest point in Europe to America, seemed likely to benefit. In 1928, Irish aviator Colonel James Fitzmaurice stated that he had spoken to politicians who viewed Galway as an ideal location for an Irish transatlantic airport. In 1935, Aillebrack near Ballyconneely was mooted as this potential site. Ultimately, it came down between Aillebrack and Rinneanna Point, Co. Clare. The latter, which coincidentally was in the constituency of then Taoiseach Éamonn de Valera, was ultimately chosen. It afterwards came to be known as Shannon Airport.

Undoubtedly, the most impressive accomplishment of the first Irish government was the Shannon Scheme in Ardnacrusha, Co. Clare, which harnessed Ireland's longest river to provide electricity to the country. It took four years and used approximately one fifth of the state's annual income to complete this massive infrastructural project. The scheme generated electricity for the national grid for the first time in October 1929. Its initial aim was to provide electricity to all urban centres of more than 500 people. Galway had some provision of electricity before this. In fact, there were a grand total of thirteen different suppliers in the county before 1929. Kylemore Castle, for example, had electric light in the nineteenth century, while several of the towns in Co. Galway benefited from private power schemes from the early 1900s. The Shannon Scheme quickly replaced these schemes in supplying Galway City and the towns in the county. Between 1929 and 1946, thirteen towns and villages across Galway were supplied directly by the Shannon Scheme. Gort, Ballinasloe, Loughrea and Galway City were the first to be connected to the grid in 1930, with other large towns, including Tuam, following close behind later in the 1930s. In 1946, with the major towns and cities connected, the rural electrification scheme was put in place. Galway was a predominantly rural county and two thirds of the houses remained in the dark. Portumna was one of the first beneficiaries of this rural-focused scheme, receiving electric light for the first time in 1947. More remote parts of Galway waited until the end of the 1950s and into the '60s for the service. Unsurprisingly, the islands off the coast of Galway were forced to wait even longer and many had to rely on a diesel generator to supply their power needs for decades. Not all people welcomed the new technology in the early days. Some older people, who had lived without electricity all their lives, refused to subscribe to the new service, which they considered unnecessary, expensive, or perhaps even dangerous. Most people were elated with the new development, however, and village parties to welcome electricity were common. It went on to change life in County Galway forever.

SOCIAL LIFE IN GALWAY

Fairs and markets remained common in the villages and towns of County Galway after independence. On fair days, many farmers dressed in their best clothes and did their business early, buying and selling cattle, sheep, pigs or horses. There was also much eating, drinking and entertainment on what was a highlight of the social calendar for many. Most fairs have died out and animals are generally sold at marts today. The Ballinasloe Fair has gone from strength to strength, however, and is now arguably the most famous fair in Ireland. Although it is largely associated with horses in the modern era, it was originally a market that sold large numbers of sheep and cattle. The origin of Ballinasloe Fair is shrouded in mystery but the town, on the eastern extremity of Galway, is a convenient central point for Connacht and the midlands. By the 1850s, the new railway stopped at Ballinasloe and the town was also the terminus of the Grand Canal, making transportation of livestock much easier and ensuring that the fair thrived over the next number of decades. An energetic committee in Ballinasloe has ensured that the fair retains its place in the calendar as one of the most important dates in the equine world, thousands continuing to descend on the town each October as they have done for centuries.

One of the few industries that flourished in Galway after independence was the illicit distillation of poteen (*poitín*), a strong homemade spirit made from potatoes. Its manufacture was a time-honoured tradition in rural areas, although keeping it a secret from the authorities was not always straightforward. Connemara was particularly renowned for the practice, with east Galway and the city buying much of the produce. Summons for distillation were a regular occurrence and stories abound of ingenious methods of concealing poteen stills in order to evade suspicion. Acclaimed playwright and novelist Brendan Behan was a regular visitor to Carraroe, an area that was known to produce poteen by the barrel-load. Despite his reputation as something of a party animal, Behan did not like poteen. He said:

> Poteen is murder. I once knew a man who drank poteen at the rate of about a couple of pints a day until he finally wasn't able to drink anymore and he got so ill that he was on his back for a fortnight before he recovered. I asked him, 'Why,' I said, 'if it makes you sick do you continue to drink it? Do you not remember the terrible hangovers you have?' 'Well no,' he said, 'because to tell you the truth when I have been off it for about a fortnight, I feel so good

that I just have to go out and celebrate and what better way than with a glass of poteen!'[21]

OTHER RECREATIONS IN GALWAY

Nightly house-to-house visitation was common in a time before television and the radio were in every home. Visits were rarely planned; people rambled here and there and called for a visit anywhere, often unannounced. Arising from casual visits such as these arose sing-songs, music-playing and dancing. Céili dancing in the country houses was popular. *Sean-nós* traditional singing and dancing was practised widely. Storytelling was also popular, many of the stories concerning the little people or other supernatural creatures. People tended to believe in ghosts at this time and there were many superstitious now largely forgotten; a child from Newcastle National School, Co. Galway, collected several superstitions held by people in the county in 1937. Among them was the belief that a man should not start any work on Saturday or cut turf between the two Holy Thursdays, and that a person should only move into a new house on a Friday. There was also a strong belief in sea monsters. Off the coast of Renvyle, it was said that a merman was spotted by two fishermen in 1938, for example, a story that featured in dozens of contemporary newspapers, including the *Times of London*. This tradition did not die out in the 1930s – as late as the 1960s there were reports of strange beasts in both Lough Fadda and Lough Auna near Clifden and in Killary Harbour.

Card playing was also popular, particularly the game of '25', called '45' in some areas. The wireless was also

21 Kelly, C. (2002), *The Grand Tour of Galway*, pp.202–203.

starting to make an impact by the 1930s, even before electricity, models running on battery power. Some would say Galway was the birthplace of the device, Italian inventor Guglielmo Marconi having pioneered radio technology at Derrigimlagh, near Clifden, in the early twentieth century. It was towards the end of the 1920s before 2RN, Ireland's national wireless broadcaster, first went on air. Initially it had limited signal and was unavailable to most Galwegians, even those lucky enough to own a receiver. Music, with or without the radio, was popular in Galway and singing, both traditional and *sean-nós*, was an admired skill. Other more modern types of music made appearances, although these generally did not meet the approval of the Catholic Church, as shown by their anti-jazz campaign in the 1930s that viewed most forms of foreign music and dance as immoral.

Songs about local themes were more acceptable to the church hierarchy and these were collected and sung regularly. Many of Galway's most famous songs are difficult to credit to any one individual and the year they were written is often impossible to ascertain. 'Connemara Cradle Song' is one example of an old Irish folk song that was written about the county, the origin of which is hard to pinpoint. Some sources have attributed the lyrics of the soothing lullaby to singer and collector of Irish ballads Delia Murphy. 'The Galway Shawl' is another song synonymous with the county and it was first published in 1936. It is based on the courtship of a man and a woman, the natural beauty of the latter being amplified by the simple Galway Shawl across her shoulders. 'The West's Awake' is a song about the county that has a definite composer, Thomas Davis. The song was written in 1843 and its lyrics go back to ancient times, speaking of the glorious defence mounted by Galwegians against outside invaders. Other famous traditional songs about Galway include 'The Shawl of Galway Grey' and 'My Connemara Rose'.

Many of these songs may have been sung around the fireplace in post-independence Galway but there are more modern songs, and ones with international appeal, about the county as well. 'The Fields of Athenry' is surely the most famous song about the Famine, written by Dubliner Pete St John in 1979. The song references the transportation of a young Athenry father who had been convicted of stealing corn to feed his starving children, a crime for which he was to be forcibly removed to Australia. The song is now an anthem for Galway GAA teams and is also sung regularly at Celtic FC and Munster rugby matches. 'Galway Girl' is the name of two famous songs, one by Ed Sheeran, and another by Mundy. There are two different songs of renown called 'Galway Bay', one of which was famously sung by Bing Crosby, while this song is also mentioned in arguably the most famous Christmas song in the world, 'Fairytale of New York'.

Cinema was another popular form of entertainment in post-independence Ireland, a cinema being advertised in Galway City as early as 1909. It provided a glimpse of a more glamorous lifestyle and by the 1930s had become wildly popular among both young and old. By that stage, there were cinemas in every town in Galway and travelling projectors visited smaller villages. The Estoria, marketed as Galway's luxury cinema, opened in November 1939 and had 776 seats and two showings a night. The Church was somewhat disapproving of this pastime and censorship in Ireland was strict. Many movies that seem tame by modern standards fell victim to the censor as they were said to 'undermine Christian standards of morality and decency'.

WEATHER PHENOMENA IN GALWAY

One facet of life that was less likely to be an issue in County Galway was the climate, which although generally wet and windy with comparatively few hours of sunshine, was usually mild and did not suffer from extreme temperatures. The hottest recorded temperature ever experienced in Galway is just 31.7 degrees, while on the other end of the scale, -11.7 was the coldest weather ever measured. Nevertheless, there have been freak weather incidents in Galway. The Great Lisbon Earthquake of 1 November 1755 destroyed much of Portugal but also created a huge tsunami that hit Ireland around three hours later. It destroyed houses on Galway's west coast, particularly around Kinvara. It also damaged the Spanish Arch in the city, while Aughinish Island, further south, was created when the huge waves washed away the narrow causeway that had previously joined it to the Galway mainland.

A more modern freak weather event occurred in early 1947 when a combination of strong winds and freezing temperatures, dropping as low as -11 and not exceeding 0 degrees on many days, struck the county. Blizzards and unprecedented snow drifts followed and there were thirty days of snow between 24 January and 16 March. Transport, communication and commerce ground to a halt and a severe lack of fuel exacerbated the situation, causing suffering and death in some cases. The mountainous inland of Connemara suffered devastation and the region was largely cut off from the outside world for much of this crisis. Roads were impassable with snow and people were imprisoned in their homes. Sheep and cattle were stranded in the snow and farmers were unable to reach them to provide them with food. Water sources were also frozen. Four miles of electricity wires near Tuam were damaged, leaving the residents of the area without electricity for more than a week. The town was also said to be completely out of milk. Fuel quickly ran out and there were reports that many householders were burning furniture to stay warm. A blizzard on 1 February was said by many to be the worst ever seen in the county and motorists were stranded on byroads all over Galway. The thaw eventually set in around St Patrick's Day, much to the relief of those trapped.

Hurricane Debbie was a second catastrophic event that occurred in Galway, although it lasted only a couple of hours. The tropical cyclone hit with little warning on the morning and afternoon of 16 September 1961 and was the biggest storm to hit the west of Ireland since the 'Night of the Big Wind' in 1839, gusts reaching an astonishing 114mph in places. Hundreds of buildings were damaged, some homes being levelled. Christ Church, the Protestant chapel in Clifden, had its west gable and part of its nave destroyed, while Cleggan Tower was extensively damaged by the fierce winds. The Jes Rowing Club in Galway City was destroyed. Newspapers, meanwhile, reported that Galway City resembled 'a bombed-out area', with multiple trees falling in Eyre Square, while Salthill fell victim to large-scale coastal flooding. Roads throughout Galway were blocked by falling trees, while countless signposts were uprooted from the ground. Reports also came in of cows and other livestock being killed by falling trees and debris, as well as of several injuries to people in the area. The storm was over within hours but electricity and phone lines were not fully restored for weeks. Miraculously, however, nobody was killed in Co. Galway, despite eighteen deaths nationwide. There have been other memorable weather fronts: a terribly cold winter in 1963 rivalled 1947, for example, while Hurricane Charley battered Galway in 1986 and caused extensive damage. The warm, dry summers of 1995 and 2018 in Co. Galway are looked back upon with great fondness, while 2002 is remembered in the county for its interminable rain.

10

THE MAKING OF MODERN GALWAY

RELIGION AND POLITICS IN GALWAY

The 1930s was a poor time economically in Galway and Fianna Fáil were granted power by a disgruntled electorate in 1932. The party was led by Éamonn de Valera and comprised many who had fought the civil war against the new state. The Galway electorate had changed utterly by then, however. All men and women over the age of 21 could now vote, and all younger voters in 1932 had not been of age when the civil war was being waged. Fianna Fáil's promise to represent the ordinary worker and to banish austerity was well received and they received five of the nine seats in the vast Co. Galway constituency in 1932, helping them to narrowly assume power from their former mortal enemies Fine Gael. De Valera had a large following and travelled the country regularly, speaking to supporters. He came to Galway on a number of occasions, including in 1934 when he spoke to 6,000 people at Clifden after arriving on horseback. He had plenty of detractors as well and the handover of power was strained. Relations between Fianna Fáil and Fine Gael (formerly called Cumann na nGaedheal), the pro-Treaty party who had been in government since the country's independence, were strained and the IRA regularly broke up Fine Gael meetings. This led to a group named the Blueshirts being founded. Modelled on Mussolini's Blackshirts, the Blueshirts had a large following in Galway and protected Fine Gael meetings. They also had fascist sympathies and on 12 December 1936, 700 men Blueshirts left Galway docks bound for Spain to fight for Franco in the Spanish Civil War.

One of the new governing party's first acts was to refuse to pay land annuities to Britain, a measure that their predecessors had agreed to in the Treaty. Britain responded by placing tariffs on Irish exports. Tit-for-tat export measures were placed upon each other's goods, until a full-scale economic war broke out, lasting six years. Combined with a worldwide economic depression, this policy left Ireland's economy in tatters and emigration from Galway soared. By the 1930s, Irish people constituted the highest number of foreign-born residents of Boston, despite our tiny population relative to other countries with histories of emigrating to the USA.

Fianna Fáil had promised efforts to curb emigration and one policy to aid this was assisted migration within Ireland. This involved the voluntary removal of families

A scene in Galway (from *One Irish Summer* by William Eleroy Curtis).

from overcrowded areas in the west to more fertile and less populated farms in the east of the country. The government also wished to spread the Irish language, which had lost its foothold in the east generations before, and the removal of native Irish speakers to superior lands in the east would help accomplish this. South Connemara along the coast was heavily populated, most farmers having a paltry few stony acres to work on. For this reason, it proved easy to attract young families from the area to travel and settle in the east. The most famous example of this transplantation was the movement of forty-one families from Connemara to the fertile lands of Co. Meath around Rath Cairn in the mid-1930s. Each family was given a new land commission house, 22 acres of land, a horse, a cow, poultry, and an allowance of 30*s* a week for one year. Large families were encouraged. The policy was a partial success and the Galway dialect of the Irish language is still spoken in Rath Cairn today. Several other transplantations from Galway, not all from Gaeltacht regions, occurred in the 1940s and '50s to counties such as Meath, Westmeath and Kildare. One of the Fianna Fáil government's other legacies was the huge numbers of social houses being built all over the county. Many of the traditional thatched cottages in the suburb of Claddagh were condemned and knocked down, for example, new social housing being built in their place.

RELIGIOUS LIFE IN GALWAY

The strong position of the Catholic Church in the new state did not change with the new government, Fianna Fáil being equally devoted to Catholicism as their predecessors. The Church saw itself as arbitrators of morality. Almost all schools and hospitals in Co. Galway were run by the

Church, some doing great work. Other Church-run institutions have a less positive legacy. Mother and Baby homes, where unmarried pregnant mothers were dispatched and sometimes held for years, were present in Co. Galway, as at Tuam, where it has recently come to light that hundreds of bodies were buried unceremoniously in an unmarked grave. There were also industrial schools in the county: at Letterfrack and Salthill for boys and at Ballinasloe for girls. These were often places of great cruelty. A small number of the children were sent here due to criminal offences they had committed, although most were orphans or simply members of families deemed by the state to be unable or unwilling to care for their welfare. Mass graves have also been found in some of these institutions, notably at Letterfrack.

Galway is home to three Roman Catholic dioceses: Tuam, Clonfert and Galway. The boundaries of most dioceses in Ireland have been in place since the year 1111, including Tuam and Clonfert. The third diocese, Galway, Kilmacduagh and Kilfenora, only came into being in 1831. More than 95 per cent of Galway residents were recorded as Roman Catholics after independence and the level of devotion to the Church was shown clearly by the massive five-day Eucharistic Congress held in Ireland in 1932. Hundreds of thousands of Catholics travelled to the capital and hundreds of events were planned in Galway to display the piety of the people. On 3 June 1932, an enormous statue of Jesus that had been carried halfway up the mountain behind Kylemore Abbey was unveiled to coincide with the Congress. Shrines and altars were also erected on roadsides throughout Galway and it was not unusual to see passersby kneeling in fervent prayer. Vatican and eucharistic flags were reportedly sold out in all shops in Co. Galway in the days before the Congress and places on trains were impossible to come by.

In 1937, Éamonn de Valera helped to draft a new constitution for the Free State that gave the Catholic Church a 'special position', although it also recognised the rights of people to practise other religions. The constitution was highly conservative, and feminist and liberal groups were generally against it. Nevertheless, it passed with 56 per cent of voters in favour. In Galway West, a whopping 74 per cent voted for the constitution, indicating the deeply conservative nature of society.

GALWAY AND THE 'EMERGENCY'

One positive development was the end of the Economic War with Britain in 1938. However, this was almost immediately followed by the Emergency, or Second World War as it was known outside Ireland. No sooner had Britain and Germany announced that they were at war than Ireland had declared its neutrality. Despite this neutral stance, it did not take long for the people of Galway to realise that they would not remain unaffected. On the first day of the war, a boat named *Athenia*, which had been sailing from Glasgow to Canada, was struck by a U-boat's torpedo. The boat began to sink and more than 100 of the 1,000 passengers perished. Fortunately, there were heroic efforts to help and the Norwegian vessel *Knute Nelson* picked up 450 shipwrecked people off the west coast of Ireland and brought them into Galway Harbour for emergency medical treatment. They were treated cordially by the people of Galway.

It also became clear immediately that the importation of goods from Britain or the Continent was about to become difficult, or impossible in some cases. The rationing of clothes, petrol, food and other items was thus deemed essential and was announced without delay. Ration books were distributed to every citizen shortly after the start of the war, although a thriving black market would soon develop. Petrol was strictly rationed and this caused hardship, the few private vehicles at the time soon put off the road. Doctors, priests and traders initially got a reasonable fuel allowance but as the war progressed there were complaints that they did not have enough to meet their needs. In February 1942, for example, Connemara experienced a three-week 'bread famine' as trader J.J. O'Malley of Westport had his fuel allowance cut from 100 to 40 gallons of petrol per month. This meant that he could no longer deliver flour to the villages of Connemara and it took a plea from the *Connacht Tribune* to the Minister for Supplies, and a heated exchange in the Dáil, before an emergency allowance was given to the trader. In the interim, it was stated that the people of Connemara were forced to eat potatoes for 'breakfast, lunch and dinner'.

Fearing food shortages, all Irish farmers were asked to plant a portion of their land with wheat, something that was more difficult in the less-arable western districts. The penalty for non-compliance was the potential seizure of land.

Nevertheless, by 1942 it was reported that many Galway farmers no longer needed imported flour and that in Aughrusmore many had successfully gone back to the old-fashioned method of milling flour with a quernstone. Rural Galway was perhaps luckier than some urban areas, with many families having access to homegrown vegetables, eggs and other foodstuffs. Another advantage unique to coastal areas of Galway was the valuable flotsam that sometimes came ashore during these war years. The cargo sometimes included rubber, timber and barrels of petrol, ether or even rum. Reporting such flotsam to the authorities was mandatory and it could be sold to the revenue, one Galway man getting £24 for a bale of rubber.

Mines were a less welcome visitor that were known to float onto Galway beaches on several occasions. Thankfully, there was no repeat of the explosion of a German barrel mine in Inverin in 1917 when nine local men were killed, although there were several mines sighted off the coast. In 1941, thousands of mackerel and pollock were stranded at high tide on beaches all around Galway. Surprisingly, locals did not view this as an easy source of food in strained times, many believing instead that it could be a bad omen of things to come. The body of at least one sailor came ashore on Renvyle Beach during the war, while the survivors of the SS *Lapwing*, torpedoed by a German U-boat, came onshore at Aillebrack after several gruelling days at sea. The living and the dead were well looked after by local people in both cases. An American plane also crash-landed at Athenry in 1943, the whole town allegedly coming out to see the aircraft. Stories also abounded of German craft being spotted off the west coast and fears of an invasion of the area seemed well-founded.

In 1940, the Local Defence Force was established and thousands of recruits enlisted and were trained to repel any attack. Dozens of local branches were formed throughout Galway in anticipation of such an invasion and a national naval reserve unit called the Maritime Insitute was also based in the county. Neutrality did not mean that all Irish people stayed out of the war. There was a cohort who believed Ireland should aid Britain in fighting the evils of Nazi Germany. Emily Anderson, Galway-born suffragette, and professor of languages at the University in Galway, worked in intelligence with the British Army. She was a fluent German speaker and a talented codebreaker, and was later awarded an OBE for her services. Many Galway-born men also served in the war for the British and America forces, including Lieutenant John F.

Ford of Killkerrin, who was killed on 21 July 1944 while fighting with the American forces. Ambrose Cosgrove of Sickeen served in the British forces, fighting in African and European conflict zones, before being killed by a sniper's bullet in Sicily in 1943.

The war, which many thought would be over quickly, dragged on for six years and the people of Galway read of the terrible butchery in their newspapers. Sometimes the war came uncomfortably close to home. Belfast was bombed, as was Dublin, the latter allegedly by mistake. By 1943, it was stated that there was almost nothing to buy in Galway shops for Christmas. Stout was hard to get and whiskey unobtainable. Tourism had long played an important role in the economic life of the city and county, particularly in the summer, but the number of visitors slowed to a trickle, although there was an influx of returned emigrants from England who came back to Galway to escape the nightly bombing campaigns of the German Luftwaffe or conscription into the British Army. There were other hardships. In the same winter, high tides and storms damaged many houses on the coast, while the social life of Galwegians was also greatly curtailed. Shortages of cigarettes, alcohol, petrol, paraffin and many other items rendered many activities too difficult to attend or organise.

There was plenty of fuel in Galway at least – east Galway had bogs aplenty, as did Connemara. Turf schemes were organised on many bogs and these provided much-needed employment. The logistics of moving this turf to the cities, which were running short of fuel having traditionally relied on imported coal, proved difficult, however, and by the middle of the war it was stated that there were thousands of tons of the fuel stored in the village of Roundstone that were too expensive to transport. Turf was also collected in lorries and built into enormous stacks in Eyre Square in

Galway City. It was believed there were 400 tons of turf there at one point.

As the war was nearing its end in the spring of 1945, another Galway connection came to light. Rumours abounded that Galway City native William Joyce, better known as Lord Haw-Haw, was in hiding in Connemara, having jumped from a German plane and landed at Ballinrobe with the aid of a parachute. Joyce was a prop-agandist for the German Reich, best known for his news bulletins from Germany that attempted to convince the British public that they were losing the war and had noth-ing to fear from a German victory. These rumours were not as outlandish as they sounded, as Joyce had an uncle living in the Clonbur district, but it eventually turned out to be little more than a tall tale. Joyce was ultimately cap-tured in Germany and hanged by the British government in 1946. He was buried in the prison yard at Wandsworth, but in August 1976 his remains were reinterred at the New Cemetery in Bohermore in Galway. The war itself ended in May 1945, to much jubilation across Galway, although rationing of many items continued in Ireland until 1951.

POST-WAR GALWAY

The biggest event in the years after the Emergency was the declaration of a republic in Ireland in 1949. Massive crowds lined the streets of Galway when Ireland finally left the British Commonwealth. This did not herald a new dawn for the county, however. There was some building of infra-structure, notably in the suburbs of Galway City that were beginning to grow. Large housing developments in areas like Mervue sprung up, a bone china factory being built in the area. The 1950s were often called the lost decade, however, and the state struggled to provide alternatives to emigration to a shrinking rural economy. Ireland lost half a million mainly young people, 16 per cent of its population, in that decade alone. Ireland was, along with East Germany, the only country in Europe to decline in population in the 1950s. Even towns with seemingly healthy populations were not always what they seemed. In the early 1950s Ballinasloe had a population of some 5,600, but 2,000 of them were patients in the mental hospital, as it was then known.

There were some green shoots of recovery for Galway under Seán Lemass in the 1960s. The discovery of lead and zinc in a mine at Tynagh in south-east Galway in the early years of the decade proved an economic boost and the town of Athenry became home to one of Ireland's leading co-op marts and a major creamery in the same decade. Galway City, as the regional capital and only city in Connacht, had a legacy of having its own university and government buildings, something that helped attract inward investment. The university had grown exponentially in the decades since its foundation and by the 1960s had gained a reputation for academic excellence in many fields. The first female engineering graduate in the world, Alice Perry, is believed to have come from there in 1906. Free secondary education was extended to all Irish children in 1967 and five years later Galway Regional Technical College, later the Atlantic Technological University, was founded, further adding to the educational potential of the city. The presence of an increasingly educated workforce ensured that much of the investment that went west as a counterbalance to Dublin and Cork was earmarked for Galway City.

This investment led to a growing population, which necessitated the building of several large housing developments on formerly rural land around the city, including

Shantalla. The Rahoon Flats were also built to the west of the city in the early 1970s and comprised 276 flats that were home to 1,100 people. On the eve of the new state, there were probably some 14,000 inhabitants in the city and its immediate environs. The population had risen exponentially by 1970, not just in the city but also in satellite towns and villages in all directions, including Barna, Moycullen, Menlo and Oranmore. Business parks such as Parkmore were also built on the outskirts and started attracting businesses away from the centre of the city and within easier reach of the county. Galway Airport began commercial operation at Carnmore, some 7km east of Galway City, in 1974 when a German businessman named Ernest Steiner built an airstrip beside his factory. At this time, with the poor road network, domestic flights from Galway were quicker and easier than driving in many cases and the future for the airport looked bright. Galway was growing more cosmopolitan and shopping opportunities were expanding. Galway Retail Park was opened in 1972 and Eyre Square Shopping Centre, Galway's first taste of the American mall experience, opened in 1987. Devotion to the Catholic Church had waned little in this time, however, and Pope John Paul II was responsible for the biggest crowd to be seen in modern Galway when on 30 September 1979 the pontiff celebrated Mass at the Galway Racecourse in front of an estimated 280,000 people. He declared, famously, 'Young people of Ireland, I love you.'

By the quincentennial celebrations of the city in 1984, Galway was unrecognisable from the small town of the previous century, although the past was never far away and at the end of the 1980s several sections of the town's medieval walls were discovered during excavations. The cityscape and outline of the streets in the city centre also remained largely identical to centuries before. The 1980s were another difficult decade in Irish history, however, and emigration from Galway was rife. Although the county's population grew between 1981 and 1986, for example, this was almost entirely due to growth in the city and its surrounds. In the areas of Clifden, Glenamaddy and Ballinasloe, there was a marked decrease as many left rural Ireland in search of an economic future. The closure of the copper mine at Tynagh in 1981 and the Tuam Sugar Plant in 1987 were two devastating blows to rural Galway's economy. Galway City suffered a similar blow when Digital, one of Ireland's biggest employers, closed its doors in 1993 and 600 people were put out of work. Hard as it was to see then, however, the fortunes of Galway were about to be transformed for the better.

GALWAY AND THE CELTIC TIGER

The Celtic Tiger was an unprecedented economic boom that transformed Ireland from one of western Europe's poorest economies to one of its richest in little over a decade. Ireland's membership of the European Union (since 1973), increasingly educated workforce and preferential corporation tax rates attracted many foreign companies looking for a European base in the early 1990s and Galway was one of the major beneficiaries, many American multinationals seeing the western city as an ideal home. Medical device companies such as Medtronic and Boston Scientific were particularly important and grew to employ workforces of thousands. The companies continue to thrive today and many employees commute from county areas. Galway is also now well-served by a motorway network from the north (M17), east (M6) and south (M18). There is also a good rail link to towns such as Athenry, Ballinasloe and Gort and an improving bus service, giving commuters from all areas of Galway the chance to work in the city while living in a more rural setting.

The county saw some improvements too, especially the Gaeltacht region of south Connemara. *Údarás na Gaeltachta* had been set up to specifically provide employment for Irish-speaking areas and several thriving factories came to the area in the Celtic Tiger era. An Irish language television service, *Telefís na Gaeilge* (later TG4), was launched in 1996, its base located at Baile na hAbhann in the Connemara Gaeltacht. The station quickly went from strength to strength and became a great showcase for the Irish language and an important employer locally. *Raidió na Gaeltachta,* based in nearby Casla, is also a huge success, having been founded in the 1970s. Rosaveel (*Ros a Mhíl*), too, has become one of the foremost Irish fishing ports, as well as the point of departure for the main ferries to the Aran Islands. Connemara even has its own air link to the islands at Inverin. Outside the Gaeltacht, other areas thrived in this era and towns such as Athenry and Oranmore were transformed from small market towns in the early 1990s to bustling hubs of employment two decades later. By the early 2000s, Galway City was quoted by several sources as the fastest-growing city in Europe and huge housing estates were springing up around the city, particularly in Knocknacarra to the west, which grew from fields and bog in the early 1980s to one of the west of Ireland's most densely populated suburbs in a little over twenty years.

Despite this industrialisation, agriculture remains an important player in County Galway. The county is home to the third highest number of sheep behind Mayo and Donegal, the animal outnumbering humans with there being 440,000 in total. It also has the third highest number of cattle at 435,000, just behind the fertile counties of the

Golden Vale, Tipperary and Cork. Many counties have a high incidence of one of these animals but the prominence of both animals in County Galway shows the diverse methods of farming that continue to play a major role in the local economy. Sheep can be found all throughout Galway, both in the mountainous west and the fertile east. Smaller farms in the west with several beef cattle also remain relatively common, while large dairy farms in the east of the county are vitally important to the local economy.

TOURISM IN MODERN GALWAY

Tourism also exploded in popularity in the 1990s and today the county receives close to 2 million visitors each year, making it the second most visited county after Dublin. Some visitors are from Galway's extensive diaspora, looking for the land of their ancestors. Others came out of curiosity to visit Galway City, which had been voted Europe's friendliest city on several occasions in the *Condé Nast* Reader Awards. The city is home to many hugely successful annual events, such as the Galway International Arts Festival, the Galway Writers' Festival and the Galway Film Fleadh, all of which attract thousands of visitors. It is also renowned for its character-filled pubs, medieval streetscapes and live music. The Galway Market, which has been ongoing for centuries, is also a magnet for tourists keen on sampling local artisan fare. Many couples who come to the city look for the renowned Claddagh Ring (or the *Fáinne Chladaigh*). The ring's origins are somewhat uncertain, although many sources attribute the first Claddagh Ring to the jeweller Richard Joyce, a goldsmith who had been kidnapped by pirates in the seventeenth century. On his release, he crafted the symbol of love and affection. The traditional Irish ring consists of two hands either side of a heart with a crown atop them all and it is now one of the most recognisable pieces of jewellery in the world.

East Galway also has a burgeoning tourism industry. Loughrea is renowned for its cathedral, its lakeside scenery and its fishing but it is also has plenty of history, the lake beside the town being home to a number of crannogs, while there are several ringforts in the vicinity as well. Tuam, too, is increasingly appreciated for its historic value, with its two cathedrals, high crosses and interesting architectural heritage. Portumna, built on the banks of Lough Derg and an ancient crossing point of Ireland's longest river, the Shannon, receives abundant water traffic and is synonymous with the Irish Workhouse Centre, opened in 2011. The centre's aim is to educate locals and tourists

The Galway Market (from *The Charm of Ireland* by Burton Egbert Stevenson).

alike about the terrible story of the Famine. Meanwhile, nearby Portumna Forest Park is a popular location for leisure. Headford and the north Galway region has long been famed for its fishing and its ecclesiastical heritage, notably Ross Erilly, a fourteenth-century friary. The southern part of Galway around Gort also boasts an array of ecclesiastical gems, including the church at Kiltiernan, reputed to be Ireland's oldest. Dunguaire Castle and the seaside village of Kinvara, gateway to Clare's rocky Burren landscape, are also popular spots to visit. This area also hosts internationally renowned festivals. The Clarinbridge Oyster Festival, which has been running since 1954, attracts visitors from all over the world, while *Crinniu na mBad* (The Gathering of the Boats) has been held in Kinvara each summer since the late 1970s and celebrates the living tradition of the sailing of beautiful Galway Hookers.

Connemara might be said to be the jewel in Galway's crown, however. It is renowned for its scenery and is home to several of the west of Ireland's top tourist attractions, including Connemara National Park, which covers more than 2,000 hectares and is home to much of the Twelve Bens mountain range. Opened in 1980 and run by the National Parks and Wildlife Service, it is one of just six national parks in the Republic of Ireland and its expanse ranges from land at sea level to mountains of more than 700m. There are also vast stretches of bogs, glittering lakes and abundant woodland, boasting all the flora and fauna of Galway's unspoiled wildernesses. Diamond Hill in the park is the most climbed mountain in Co. Galway. From its summit, climbers can see in every direction for miles, including Ireland's only fjord, Killary Harbour.

Travellers to Connemara also come in their droves to Kylemore Abbey, a place brimming with history. Originally called Kylemore Castle, it was constructed in an isolated

Kylemore Abbey.

spot in the Connemara mountains in 1868. The builder was one Mitchell Henry, a wealthy businessman and soon-to-be MP, who arrived to the spot on honeymoon with his wife Margaret. Margaret immediately fell in love with the place, and after the castle's construction, it was supplied with electricity and fabulous gardens with exotic plants. The pair lived there happily for six years until Margaret died in 1874 during a holiday in Egypt. Her body was returned to Ireland and laid to rest in a specially built mausoleum. The castle eventually ended up in the hands of the Benedictine nuns in around 1920. They soon changed its name to Kylemore Abbey and opened a boarding school for girls. In 2010, the school was closed and Kylemore Abbey and Victorian Walled Gardens became one of Ireland's premier tourist attractions, welcoming upwards of half a million visitors each year.

Other visitors to Connemara come to learn Irish, to visit the islands off the coast or to fish in the world-renowned lakes. Still others come to marvel at the Connemara pony, Ireland's only indigenous breed of horse, famed for its athleticism and even temperament. The Clifden Show each August attracts lovers of the animal from all over the world.

ARTS, CULTURE AND SPORTING GALWAY

PAINTERS, PLAYWRIGHTS AND FILM STARS

A county is far more than its economy and Galway is well-known for its contribution to modern art, literature, culture and sport. In the state's formative decades, artists flocked to Connemara. Armagh native Charles Lamb was so moved by the landscape in Galway that in the 1930s he settled in Carraroe and painted local life while running a summer painting school. Harry Kernoff, Jack B. Yeats and Maurice McGonigal were others who got inspiration from Galway City and county and have left a rich artistic legacy. The performing arts are also important to Galway and the city has several theatres, including the world-renowned Druid Theatre and *An Taibhdhearc*, which was opened on Middle Street in 1928 and was designated Ireland's national theatre for the Irish language. Its first production was *Diarmuid and Gráinne*, indicating its intention to highlight Irish history and culture. Galway native Siobhán McKenna was one of the foremost actors who appeared on stage here, and she went on to appear in several Hollywood movies. Walter Macken was also a regular actor and playwright at the venue, and is now regarded among Galway's most famous writers. Macken produced seventy-six plays in less than a decade but by the end of the 1950s he had turned his attention to writing novels, including 1959's *Seek the Fair Land*. This was followed by *The Silent People* (1962) and *The Scorching Wind* (1964). The novels were simple and unsentimental, examining starkly the difficult lives of the poor in the west of Ireland. They proved hugely popular. Theatres can be found outside the city as well. The Mall Theatre in Tuam and the Town Hall Theatre in Ballinasloe have a long history of hosting quality live events.

Several important films have used Galway as their backdrop. *Riders to the Sea,* based on J.M. Synge's play of the same name, was filmed here in 1935. Most famously, perhaps, was *The Quiet Man* (1952), which was filmed on location in Leam, near Oughterard, where the famous Quiet Man Bridge can be seen. Other scenes feature Lettergesh Beach, where the horse racing scene was filmed, and Ballyglunin, near Tuam, where Castletown Railway Station was situated. Lovers of the film still visit Galway in their droves. *The Field* (1990) was another internationally renowned film that used Galway as a backdrop, the village of Leenane playing host to the famous character Bull McCabe. Several Galway actors have also made their mark. Peter O'Toole, the renowned stage and film actor, often claimed to have been born in Galway. His father was certainly from the county and the ashes of the *Lawrence of Arabia* star were scattered near Clifden. Pauline McGlynn, known by many as the character Mrs Doyle in *Father Ted*, grew up in Galway and has gone on to have a stellar career appearing in *Angela's Ashes*, *Doctor Who* and *The Young Offenders*. Nicola Mary Coughlan, who grew up in Oranmore, is another up-and-coming actress, best known as Claire Devlin from *Derry Girls*.

POETS AND AUTHORS

Poets and writers have also gravitated towards Galway, and indeed there are many eminent examples who were born and reared in the county. Máirtín Ó Cadhain, a

Spiddal native, was born in 1904 and was a principal in various Galway schools before losing his job due to his membership of the IRA. Imprisoned during the Second World War, Ó Cadhain had already written several collections by the time he was released. *Cré na Cille* was his most famous novel. Many of his stories dealt with the lot of the rural poor in his native county. Liam O'Flaherty (b. 1896) was a native of the Aran Islands and was also a radical. He believed that communism would be the ideal form of government in a newly independent Ireland. O'Flaherty wrote his most famous work *The Informer* in 1925, a novel about the Dublin underground in the aftermath of the civil war. Possibly Galway's most lauded author, however, is Padraic Ó Conaire. Ó Conaire was from Galway City but grew up in Rosmuc. He published more than 400 short stories, including '*M'Asal Beag Dubh*' ('My Little Black Ass'), many while living in London. Many of these stories discussed matters such as prostitution and alcoholism, issues that were taboo in Ireland of the time. He returned to his home country during the First World War and began to drink heavily, dying destitute in Dublin in 1928. Seven years later, a statue of Ó Conaire was unveiled in Eyre Square and was for many decades a hugely significant marker in the city.

Galway continues to produce highly regarded poets and authors. Rita Ann Higgins is one of the county's premier poets and playwrights. A native of Ballyrbit in the eastern suburbs of Galway City, Higgins' poems often deal with the inequalities that persist in modern Ireland. Mary O'Malley, a native of Ballyconneely, has also shown herself to be a poet of great ability. The president of Ireland, Michael D. Higgins, has also called Galway home for most of his life and is well known for his poetry, which deals with a myriad of social and cultural issues.

SPORT IN MODERN GALWAY

Sport has continued to play a defining role in the culture of modern Galway. The Galway Races combines tradition and modernity and is arguably Ireland's most celebrated race meeting, the week-long festival attracting huge crowds. The first official meeting at Ballybrit Racecourse was held on 17 August 1864 with 40,000 spectators in attendance. The spectators travelled by railway, on horseback and by foot, many coming from far-flung places. The Galway Plate, with a purse of one hundred sovereigns for the winner, was the main event. The day was a great success, socially as well as in terms of sport, and many of the wealthiest denizens of the west of Ireland could be found among the attendees. The races grew in scope and style with each passing year and quickly established themselves as a fixture on the horse racing calendar. Hunting with horses has also been hugely popular in the fertile eastern tracts of Galway for centuries, the Galway Blazers hunting club being among the longest established in Ireland. The club also continues to run events to this day.

Gaelic football also blossomed after independence and Galway's county team has won a total of nine all-Ireland football titles, leaving them third place in the roll of honour nationally. Their first all-Ireland was in 1925, followed by further successes in 1934, 1938 and 1956. A purple patch in the 1960s saw the county becoming one of the few to win the title three times in a row, in 1964, 1965 and 1966. Another brilliant generation in the late 1990s and early 2000s saw Galway winning the title in 1998 and 2001, losing out in two other keenly contested finals. Several club teams, most notably Corofin, have won all-Ireland club titles as well, marking Galway out as one of the most successful counties in Ireland in terms of the sport. The women's football scene is also very strong in Galway and the county won its sole all-Ireland title in 2004 to much celebration.

The Galway hurling team have also enjoyed some memorable successes, finally winning its first all-Ireland in 1923 after beating Limerick 7-3 to 4-5. Their most fruitful period was in the 1980s, when they won the first all-Ireland of that decade before winning further titles in 1987 and 1988. Galway won hurling's biggest prize for the fifth time in 2017, beating Waterford 0-26 to 2-17 in front of more than 82,000 people at Croke Park. Their underage teams are also very successful, Galway topping the roll of honour in the minor grade, while several Galway clubs have claimed the honours in the club championship. Camogie, similar to hurling but played by women, is also exceptionally popular and Galway have won a total of four camogie all-Irelands, most recently in 2021.

Soccer has also been popular in Galway for generations, particularly in the city, and Galway United has flown the flag for the county since its foundation in 1937 as Galway Rovers. They play their home games at Éamonn Deacy Park, formerly Terryland Park, and were crowned winners of the FAI Cup in 1991 in what is probably their greatest achievement. They have also appeared in European competitions on several occasions. Club soccer is also popular, with most parishes being represented by one club in the local league, while the city is home to several highly ranked junior sides. Ryan Manning is among the Galwegians who have played for the Irish international soccer team, while Niamh Fahey from Killannin is among the highest-capped players on the women's national side.

Rugby, too, has had an imprint on sporting life in Galway through both Connacht, the province, and several clubs, most notable among them Galwegians, Buccaneers and Corinthians. Connacht Rugby began all the way back in 1885 when it was founded by several natives of the province with a huge interest in the game. The Sportsground was opened in Galway City in 1927 and remains the home of Connacht Rugby to this day. Connacht was threatened with extinction by the Irish Rugby Football Union in 2003 but a grassroots movement of supporters ensured that the province lived to fight another day, and they were vindicated when Connacht went on to win the Pro-12 Cup in 2016, surely their finest achievement. Galway players such as Ciarán Fitzgerald, Eric Elwood and Tiernan O'Halloran have gone on to represent their country with distinction.

Galway has even had some Olympic success. Michael Kelly was among the first, winning two gold medals in the 1920 Olympics in Antwerp, despite not representing his home country. Kelly was a native of Attymon, Co. Galway, but emigrated to America in around 1888 when he was 16 years old. A sergeant in the US Army, Kelly was known for his excellence in shooting and was chosen for the US Olympic Team. Francis Barrett, a member of the travelling community who have called Galway their home for centuries, was the first from the community to represent Ireland in the Olympics when he travelled to the Atlanta Games in 1996. He was honoured with the task of carrying the flag and performed brilliantly in the Games. At the 2020 Tokyo Olympics, which were deferred for a year due to Covid-19, Fiona Murtagh and Aifric Keogh, both natives of Galway, won bronze medals as part of the Women's Coxless Four. This was Irish rowing's first women's Olympic Medal.

AFTERWORD

GALWAY CHANGED UTTERLY

Socially, Galway has changed utterly in the last four decades and has played its part in a gradual liberalisation of national laws. Contraception, which had been banned in Ireland since 1935, was legalised at the beginning of the 1980s. In 1993, homosexuality was decriminalised, while two years later a referendum on divorce was held. Galway, due to its rural make-up, tended to be more conservative that areas such as Dublin, and Galway West rejected the motion, with just 48 per cent in favour, while the overwhelmingly rural Galway East had one of the lowest percentages in favour at just 35 per cent.

The motion passed narrowly regardless, a clear sign that the Catholic Church was beginning to lose much of its power, partly due to several scandals. One of these involved the Bishop of Galway, Éamonn Casey, who was found in 1992 to have fathered a child with a woman named Annie Murphy and afterwards given her thousands of pounds of church funds. Far worse was to follow when widespread tales of clerical physical and sexual abuse were uncovered, Galway institutions such as the industrial school in Letterfrack being prominent.

Tuam Mother and Baby Home, which was closed in the early 1960s, also came to the attention of the country when mass graves were discovered in a disused septic tank. The demographics of Galway have also changed utterly in the same time frame, according to the most recent census of 2021. The population of County Galway remains around 75 per cent Catholic, although atheists are a growing minority. There are also small numbers of members of other faiths, including Protestantism, Islam, Hinduism and Judaism in a more diverse population, with 12 per cent of respondents now recording their home country as being somewhere other than Ireland.

Modern Galway is, on the whole, a far wealthier place than in decades past but there remain challenges that would have been difficult to foresee in years gone by, the property market among them. Two thirds of adults in Galway state that they own their own home, a seemingly healthy figure but a number that is plummeting among younger generations in an increasingly difficult market. Galway can be divided into three regions in terms of housing. Accommodation in the city and the suburbs, as well as outlying towns with good links to the railway or motorway such as Athenry and Oranmore, is in huge demand and providing supply is proving a challenge. These areas have experienced strong growth and although it took a hit in the financial crash of 2008, it has bounced back strongly. The more rural areas in Galway, particularly the north-east of the county around Ballymoe and Williamstown, are far more affordable, among the cheapest in Ireland in some cases, as the area offers poor connectivity to larger urban areas and little in the way of industry. The Covid pandemic saw a shift in working practices, however, and now 30 per cent of the county's workforce do at least a portion of their work from home, something that has seen young families moving back to rural areas and may level out prices in the future. Connemara is the third region. Its properties, particularly those with access to the coast, are in demand as second homes for wealthy investors. Many older houses are snapped up and modernised, money being little object. There is also little long-term stock as many cottages are rented on the short-term tourist market. Although lucrative in the short term, this has proven disastrous for the local population, which is declining year on year, young couples unable to afford to compete with outside interests.

Galway City's location continues to bring its own challenges in the modern day as well. Sitting between two large bodies of water, Lough Corrib and the Atlantic Ocean, leaves little room for expansion without urban sprawl to the east and west and there has been little political appetite to build upwards. Much of the industrial area of the city lies to the east of the river, while residential areas on the west, such as Knocknacarra, also continue to grow, placing increasing pressure on the four bridges across the River Corrib and leading to traffic chaos at peak times.

Heated debates on the solutions to these issues are being discussed in the corridors of power, both locally and nationally, and city planners are deadlocked on whether a bypass and an extra bridge would alleviate the problem or if improved public transport would be preferable for the best vision for Galway in a more climate-conscious future. Regardless of what the ultimate choice is, it is likely that the resourceful people of Galway will continue to work hard to make sure the county thrives and remains an example to Ireland of a diversified economy with an eye on both its proud heritage and its bright future.

Galway is a county that is very much on an upward trajectory and third-level education also continues to be a draw for people from the surrounding counties to come to Galway, and not just the city. There are now branches of the Atlantic Technological University in various rural parts of the county, including the Woodwork College in Letterfrack and the Agricultural College in Mountbellew, while the National University of Ireland Galway (NUIG) has several campuses outside the city, including at Carna specialising in the Irish language. The population of County Galway was dropping steadily for well over a century after the Famine, a slide that has been completely arrested in the last forty years. Today, the economy is booming, the arts sector is vibrant, tourism is ever-growing and there are now nearly 280,000 people living within the borders of the county. We have come a long way.

SELECT BIBLIOGRAPHY

PRIMARY SOURCES

Bureau of Military History Witness Statements
Census Reports 1831/1841/1851/1881/1901/1911/2021
Congested Districts Board – Baseline Reports for Galway
Down Survey, 1658
Folklore Commission, 1937
Griffith's General Valuation of Rateable Property in Ireland, 1855
Irish Landowner's Census, 1876
Maps: Pinkerton (1813), Arrowsmith (1844), Griffith (1855)
Newspapers: *An Claidheamh Soluis, Connacht Tribune, Freeman's
    Journal, Galway Express, Galway Observer, Tuam Herald*
Ordnance Survey: National Townland and Historical Map Viewer
Petty Sessions Records

CONTEMPORARY PUBLICATIONS
AND SECONDARY SOURCES

Ashworth, W., 1851, *The Saxon in Ireland: or an Englishman's
    ramble through Connacht and Munster during the summer of
    1833*, London: J. Murray.
Barrow, J., 1835, *A Tour Round Ireland, Through the Sea-coast
    Counties, in the Autumn of 1835*, Ann Arbor: University of
    Michigan.
Becker, B., 1881, *Disturbed Ireland: Being the Letters written during
    the Winter of 1880–81*, London: MacMillan and Co.
Breathnach, C., 2005, *The Congested Districts Board of Ireland,
    1891–1923: Poverty and Development in the West of Ireland*,
    Dublin: Four Courts Press.

Da Latocnaye, C., 1797, *A Frenchman's Walk through Ireland*, Belfast: McCaw.

Dutton, H., 1824, *A Statistical and Agricultural* Survey *of the* County *of Galway*, Ballycastle: Clachan.

Finnegan, P., 2014, *Loughrea: That Den of Infamy. The Land War in Co. Galway 1879–82*, Dublin: Four Courts Press.

Gwynn, S., 1909, *A Holiday in Connemara*, London: Methuen and Company.

Hardiman, J., 1820, *The History of the Town and the County of the Town of Galway from the earliest Period to the Present Time*, Dublin: Folds.

Kavanagh, J., 2021, *The Irish Assassins: Conspiracy, Revenge and the Murder that Stunned an Empire*, Glasgow: Grove Press.

Kelly, C., 2002, *The Grand Tour of Galway*, Cork: Cailleach.

Lewis, S., 1837, *A Topographical Directory of Ireland*, London: S. Lewis Collection.

Mansfield, M.F. & B.M., 1904, *Romantic Ireland*, Boston: Page & Co.

McNally, M., 2009, *Ireland 1649–52: Cromwell's Protestant Crusade*, Oxford: Osprey Publishing.

Melvin, P., 2012, *Estates and Landed Society in Galway*, Dublin: Edmond Burke.

Moffet, F., 1985, *I also am of Ireland*, London: British Broadcasting Corporation.

Nicholson, A., 1847, *Ireland's Welcome to the Stranger*, New York: Baker and Scribner.

O'Donovan, J., 1839, *Letters Relevant to the Antiquities of the County of Galway*.

O'Dowd, M., 2000, 'Women and Paid Work in Rural Ireland c.1500–1800', Bernadette Whelan (ed.), *Women and Paid Work in Ireland 1500–1930*, pp.18–31.

O'Flaherty, R., 1684, *A Chorographical Description of West or H-Iar Connacht*, Jerusalem: Nabu.

O'Gaora, C., 2011, *On the Run*, Translation of *Mise*, edited by Ó hAodha, M. & O'Donnell, R., Dublin: Mercier.

Ross, M. & Somerville, E., 1895, *Through Connemara in a Governess Cart*, London: Virago.

Spellisey, S., 1999, *The History of Galway, City and County*, Limerick: Celtic Bookshop.

St John, O., 1614, *A Description of Connaught*, London: Virtuatem.

Synge, J.M., 1911, *Travels in Wicklow, West Kerry and Connemara*, Dublin: Maunsel & Co.

Villiers-Tuthill, K., 1986, *Beyond the Twelve Bens: A History of Clifden and District 1860–1923*, Clifden: Connemara Girl Publications.

Wilde, W., 1867, *Wilde's Lough Corrib: Its Shores and Islands*, Dublin: McGlashan & Gill.

Walford, T., 1818, *The Scientific Tourist through Ireland*, London: Booth.

Woodham-Smith, C., 1962, *The Great Hunger: The Story of the Potato Famine of the 1840s*, Alexandria: Oldtown Books.

INDEX